Celebrate!

An Anti-Bias Guide to Including
HOLIDAYS
in Early Childhood Programs

SECOND EDITION

Celebrate!

An Anti-Bias Guide to Including
HOLIDAYS
in Early Childhood Programs

SECOND EDITION

JULIE BISSON

With a New Foreword by Louise Derman-Sparks

Redleaf Press®
www.redleafpress.org
800-423-8309

Published by Redleaf Press
10 Yorkton Court
St. Paul, MN 55117
www.redleafpress.org
© 1997, 2017 by Julie Bisson

Cover design by Jim Handrigan
Interior design by Amy Fastenau
Typeset in New Century Schoolbook, McCracken, Trade Gothic
Printed in the United States of America

Library of Congress Cataloging-in-Publication Data
Names: Bisson, Julie, 1963- author.
Title: Celebrate! : an anti-bias guide to including holidays in early
   childhood programs / Julie Bisson ; foreword by Louise Derman-Sparks.
Description: St. Paul, MN : Redleaf Press, 2017.
Identifiers: LCCN 2016017147 (print) | LCCN 2016018351 (ebook) | ISBN
   9781605544533 (paperback) | ISBN 9781605544540 (ebook)
Subjects: LCSH: Holidays--Study and teaching (Early childhood)--United
   States. | Early childhood education--United States--Activity programs. |
   BISAC: EDUCATION / Inclusive Education. | EDUCATION / Preschool &
   Kindergarten. | SOCIAL SCIENCE / Holidays (non-religious). | EDUCATION /
   Teaching Methods & Materials / General.
Classification: LCC GT4803.A2 B57 2017 (print) | LCC GT4803.A2 (ebook) | DDC
   394.26--dc23
LC record available at https://lccn.loc.gov/2016017147

Printed on acid-free paper   U21-11

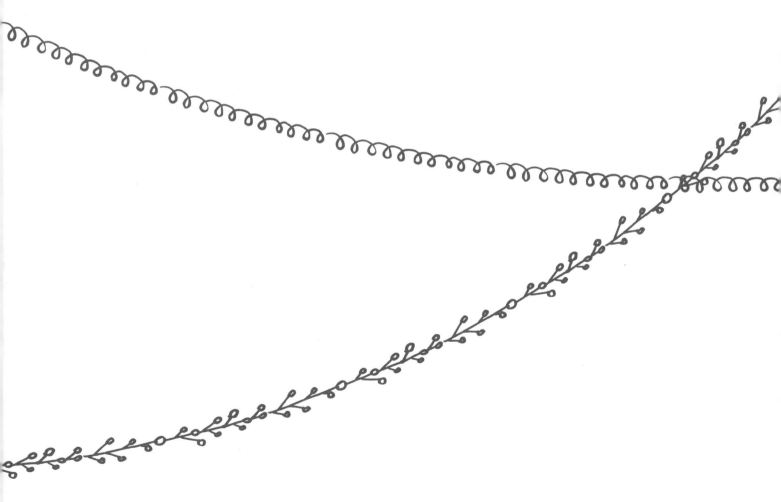

In memory of my grandmother, Armida Coppola Rotondo,
who really loved to celebrate

Contents

Foreword to the Second Edition by Louise Derman-Sparks   xi

Foreword to the First Edition by Louise Derman-Sparks   xiv

Acknowledgments   xvii

Introduction to the Second Edition   1

Introduction to the First Edition   2

PART ONE
Rethinking Holidays in the Classroom

1   The Holiday Question Has Become More Complex   9

The United States Has Changed   9

Complexities and Differing Perspectives   12

Multiple Perspectives Provide an Opportunity to Come Together   13

Rethinking Holidays in the Classroom   19

Why Celebrate Holidays in the Classroom?   22

How We Begin the Dialogue   25

PART TWO
Creating Successful Holiday Activities in Your Classroom

2   Use Developmentally Appropriate Practice   31

Review Children's Developmental Stages   32

Work with Children   33

Keep Holiday Activities in Check   35

Choose Appropriate Content   38

3   Reflect All Children's Experiences   43

Choose Activities That Reflect Home   43

Work Sensitively with Families   45

Create Balance   45

Avoid Balance Traps   47

4 Consider Religion   51
   Consider Your Own Perspective   51
   Monitor Your Own Responses   52
   Identify Your Program Type   52
   Consult Your Program's Philosophy   54
   Reflect on Your Goals   54
   Work with Families   54
   Don't Treat Religions as Homogeneous   55
   When Families Disagree   55
   Choose Your Approach   56
   Consider Issues of Accuracy and Balance   60

5 Address Stereotypes and Commercialism   61
   Understand Stereotypes   62
   Address Holiday Stereotypes   63
   Talk with Families   65
   Address Commercialism   65
   Respond to Families' Circumstances   67
   Help Children Stand Up to Bias   67

**6 Meet the Needs of Families Who Don't Want
    Their Children to Participate**   69
   Examine Your Own Feelings   70
   Dialogue with Families   70
   Provide Information   71
   Ask Questions   71
   Recheck Your Emotions   72
   Provide Different Options   73
   Communicate with Other Families   75
   Support Children   75

PART THREE
Plan and Implement Changes

7 Assess Your Situation   81
   Understand Your Own Perspective   81
   Think about Your Own Position   82
   Evaluate Your Home/School Relationships   83
   Let Your Program's Stated Vision and Values Pave the Way   84
   Lead with Values   85
   Acknowledge the Challenges of Collaboration   87

8   Determine Your Program's Goals for Holidays   89

Consider Possible Goals   89

Consult Your Program's Goals   92

Think about the Children and Families in Your Setting   92

Reflect and Review   93

9   Develop Your Holiday Policy   95

Include Everyone Who Wants to Be Included   96

Choose a Method   96

Set Your Own Ground Rules   97

Outline Your Policy   98

Periodically Evaluate Your Policy   104

10   Identify Holidays to Include   107

Gather Information from Families   107

Select Your Methods   108

Support Reluctant Families   112

Review Your Information about Families   112

Find Out about Program Requirements   113

Add Your Own Choices   114

Evaluate Your List   116

11   Introduce Unfamiliar Holidays   119

Strengthen Children by Including Unfamiliar Holidays   119

Consider Children's Development   120

Consider the Community Context   120

Use a Diagram to Help You Decide   122

Include Unfamiliar Holidays   126

12   Assess Your Holiday Activities   131

Meet to Review Your Activities   131

Plan for Improvement   132

13   Putting It All Together: Holidays in Three Classrooms 135

PART FOUR
Resources

Appendix A: Further Reading   149

Children's Resources   149

Adults' Resources   151

Appendix B: Sample Policy and Planning Documents 157
    Willow Child Care Center Holiday Policy 158
    Epiphany Early Learning Preschool Holiday Policy 162
    Sample Holiday Evaluation Questionnaire for Families 169
    Sample Family Questionnaire about Holidays 170
    Holiday Practices Improvement Plan 172

References 173

Foreword

FOREWORD TO THE SECOND EDITION
by Louise Derman-Sparks

Including holidays in the curriculum has long been a staple of early childhood programs. These activities tended to be simplified versions of mainstream celebrations such as Halloween, Thanksgiving, Christmas, Valentine's Day, Easter, and Mother's and Father's Days. Programs proceeded on an unspoken assumption that all families of the children in the program celebrated them. Holiday activities often relied on a combination of teacher-made and commercially purchased materials. These were taken off the shelf for the celebration and then put away for the following year, regardless of the makeup of the children and families in any given year.

When awareness about the realities of cultural and family diversity in ECE programs began to grow, holiday activities quickly became a focal point. Adding new holidays to the ones already regularly celebrated seemed to be an "easy" way to bring diversity into a program's curriculum. As before, many teachers continued to use commercial materials, while some asked families to help them introduce the holidays they celebrated at home—especially ones new to the staff.

However, as early childhood programs served increasingly diverse groups of children and families, it also became increasingly clear that using holidays to *respectfully* recognize and teach about diversity is *not* simple or easy. In 1979, *Young Children* published an article titled "Beyond 'Ten Little Indians' and Turkeys: Alternative Approaches to Thanksgiving" (Ramsey, 28–51). This pioneering piece called on early childhood educators to think critically about the biased messages and one-sided view of history embedded in the way the Thanksgiving story was typically taught. In 1987, Patricia G. Ramsey more fully developed her critical analysis, writing, "When holidays are the sole or main focus of a multicultural curriculum, they become token gestures rather than authentic representations of cultural diversity" (79).

Similarly, *Anti-Bias Curriculum: Tools for Empowering Young Children* (Derman-Sparks & ABC Task Force 1989) and *Anti-Bias Education for Young Children and Ourselves* (Derman-Sparks & Edwards 2010) put forward critical points about the connection between holidays and fostering diversity and fairness in early childhood education. Concerns included: (1) There is danger in oversimplifying and misrepresenting families' cultures when relying on holidays as the primary vehicles for children to learn about diversity; (2) acting as if all families celebrate the same holidays, including those of the dominant or mainstream American culture, ignores the realities of diversity; (3) requiring children to celebrate mainstream holidays as if they were their own disregards and disrespects their families' cultures; (4) certain mainstream holidays communicate misinformation and biases towards some groups of people; and (5) the commercialization of holiday celebrations promotes materialism and competition among children and "reinforces the idea that a person is worth what she or he is worth" financially (Ramsey 1987, 81).

These critiques sparked necessary discussions about holiday activities among early childhood educators. Consequently, several programs chose to respond to these issues by declaring a No-Holiday policy. But this strategy generated its own problems, as many teachers and families disagreed with it. A no-holiday approach also loses the benefits holiday activities have if they're used appropriately.

Then, the 1998 publication of the first edition of *Celebrate! An Anti-Bias Guide to Enjoying Holidays in Early Childhood Programs* offered an insightful alternative to the no-holiday solution. A significant contribution to the evolving anti-bias education approach, it advocated for staff to engage in critical thinking and creative problem solving about ways to include holidays as part of a program's curriculum. And, as Julie Olsen Edwards and I wrote in *Anti-Bias Education for Young Children and Ourselves* (2010), the central point in the holiday debate is "not deciding 'do I or don't I include holidays in my curriculum?'; it is about how to ground whatever holiday activities you do in the principles of anti-bias education" (135–136). This means always paying attention to children's identities and diversity, critical thinking about fairness/justice, and taking part in actions to create fairness.

Nevertheless, teachers and directors continue to show their perplexity about holiday activities in the curriculum. Frequent questions such as *If we use an anti-bias approach, are we allowed to do holidays?*; *How do we include holidays without offending anyone?*; *If I celebrate one holiday, do I have to celebrate all of them?*; and *How do I eliminate commercialism?* reflect core confusion about how to use holiday activities fairly.

It is a constructive sign that questions like these are being asked. At the same time, the fact that so many early childhood educators remain unsure about how to proceed indicates that the holiday issue has deep roots. For example, here is one early childhood teacher speaking about her struggle:

"Changing how I do Christmas was hard for me, because Christmas was such a big thing in my life. It was hard for me to step back and realize that what I was doing in my class was for me. But I do not want to hurt any of my children, so I did accept that I had to make some changes" (Derman-Sparks & Edwards 2010, 137).

Taking on this challenging task thoughtfully is doable. It is possible to find solutions to the questions so many educators raise. It is possible to generate new policy and strategies that integrate holiday activities into programs, while also honoring diversity and anti-bias principles. Effective new strategies for including holiday activities in curriculum exist in many childhood programs throughout our country.

The second edition of *Celebrate! An Anti-Bias Guide to Including Holidays in Early Childhood Programs!* provides wonderful tools for program leaders and teachers who desire to either initiate or strengthen their use of holidays in the context of anti-bias values. Its expanded content and new organization insightfully reflect what Julie Bisson has learned over the many years since the publication of her book's first edition. You will find a wealth of information, analysis, and strategies for creating holiday policy, as well as activities that respect family diversity, anti-bias principles, and developmentally appropriate guidelines.

One of the exciting new elements of this second edition is the discussion in part 1, which goes deeply into the fundamental issues underlying positions about holidays in the curriculum. This is an important contribution to the early childhood care and education field's discourse about what is involved in honoring family diversity. Part 2 is another useful new section, offering concrete guidelines and strategies for developing and implementing holiday activities with children. Part 3 continues the discussion about generating program holiday polices that reflect respect for diversity and anti-bias values. It also incorporates lessons from the experiences of programs that have developed and implemented new holiday polices.

Every early childhood care and education program will grow their work by taking seriously and applying the ideas in this book.

References

Derman-Sparks, Louise, and ABC Task Force. 1989. *Anti-Bias Curriculum: Tools for Empowering Young Children.* Washington, DC: NAEYC.

Derman-Sparks, Louise, and Julie Olsen Edwards. 2010. *Anti-Bias Education for Young Children and Ourselves.* Washington, DC: NAEYC.

Ramsey, Patricia G. 1979. "Beyond 'Ten Little Indians' and Turkeys: Alternative Approaches to Thanksgiving." *Young Children.* September 1989, 28–51.

Ramsey, Patricia G. 1987. *Teaching and Learning in a Diverse World: Multicultural Education for Young Children.* New York: Teachers College Press.

FOREWORD TO THE FIRST EDITION
by Louise Derman-Sparks

In my workshops and conversations about anti-bias education with early childhood practitioners throughout the country, the "holiday question" invariably comes up. The many-faceted issues connected to the topic are not only of intellectual interest; they also spark strong emotions that shape the conversations—even when the people involved are not aware this is happening.

Holidays matter deeply to people. They represent a host of experiences, feelings, connections, and memories of family and close friends; many of which are warm and positive, some of which are filled with anxiety, anger, or pain. Consequently, asking people to rethink how and why they have been using holiday activities in their early childhood programs is a much more complex and difficult task than it may first appear. It isn't surprising that considerable confusion characterizes where many teachers are on this volatile issue.

Moreover, certain basic misconceptions cloud the very necessary dialogue about the role holidays play in an anti-bias curriculum for young children. The most prevalent misconception is that an anti-bias approach means the elimination of all holidays from the curriculum. In fact, *Anti-Bias Curriculum: Tools for Empowering Young Children*, the book I wrote with the ABC Task Force, has an entire chapter devoted to a discussion about holidays. It does not say that people should stop all holiday activities in their educational program. It does raise many questions about how we have used holidays in the past as the focus of multicultural activities and about the ways we have presented and involved children in holiday activities. The primary message of the chapter about holidays is to encourage early childhood educators to rethink and make changes as necessary in their practice.

Unfortunately, instead of taking on the challenging—and possibly daunting—task of rethinking their practice, some people have opted for a "no-holiday" policy. This solution only causes further problems. It deprives children and families of a potentially enriching aspect of early childhood care and education; it deprives staff of the stretching and growing conversations essential to rethinking their holiday policy and initiating new approaches. The no-holiday solution also results in some individuals unfairly holding the anti-bias approach responsible for policies that it neither suggests nor upholds.

Another source of confusion about holidays is the anti-bias book's critique of the form of multicultural curriculum we label the "tourist approach." As part of our criticism, we point to the overuse of holidays as the primary strategy for introducing children to cultural diversity. Because, by definition, holidays are special days in all people's culture, over-reliance on holiday activities results in children not learning about the daily life of people different from themselves and thus prevents them from understanding the diverse ways people live out their shared human needs. Incorporating holiday activities as one strategy for respecting and learning about human diversity is appropriate. However, using holidays exclusively to teach about diversity does become "tourist" curriculum!

The position the anti-bias book takes on so-called national holidays—that is, those treated in child care and school settings as equally meaningful for all American children—has also sparked considerable disequilibrium and, in some cases, hostility. Nevertheless, how to address holidays such as Thanksgiving, Christmas, Easter, or Mother's Day within an anti-bias perspective does require serious rethinking. Each of these holidays represents the cultural/religious way of life and view of history of a considerable part of the population of the United States—but not of all. Many people do not consider these holidays central to their cultural or religious group's way of life. Not all groups subscribe to the view of history as expressed, for example, in the traditional Thanksgiving story. Increasing numbers of families do not fit easily into the make-one-gift tradition of Mother's Day.

This reality poses a core dilemma to educators who wish to create a democratic and inclusive early childhood program that nurtures all children in relation to their family context. How do we carry out our professional responsibility to authentically and sensitively include the cultural perspectives and life experiences of all the families whose children we serve, while also fostering all children's emotional, cognitive, and behavioral abilities to effectively and fairly interact with people different from themselves? Both responsibilities are essential to our nation's healthy survival. We cannot disparage, ignore, or inaccurately reflect some groups in favor of others.

Yet, to some people, respectful inclusion of any other group's cultural or historic perspective in the curriculum is considered a denial of their own rights. In other words, to some, "If it is not my way, then I am being victimized." As professionals, we know how to work productively with the "egocentrism" of preschoolers who assume their views are shared by everyone else and who cry "not fair" when they want the bike someone else is riding at the time. We are not made anxious by having to do conflict resolution and problem solving about sharing and taking turns with children—indeed we do this on a regular basis. But most have yet to effectively work with the conflicting and frequently ethnocentric views and needs of adults, whether they are our colleagues, staff, or the adult members of the families we serve.

Yet this is exactly what we must learn how to do. *Celebrate! An Anti-Bias Guide to Including Holidays in Early Childhood Programs* provides the tools for addressing the "holiday question" in new, creative, and effective ways. It does not solve the problems; rather, it gives you strategies for solving them yourself in collaboration with staff and families. There is no one "right" way for incorporating holiday activities within an anti-bias approach. What is "right" or meaningful for the group of children and families you serve and the teachers who bring curriculum to life can only be decided collaboratively by the people involved. This book will help you do so if you have the courage, commitment, and persistence to make it happen.

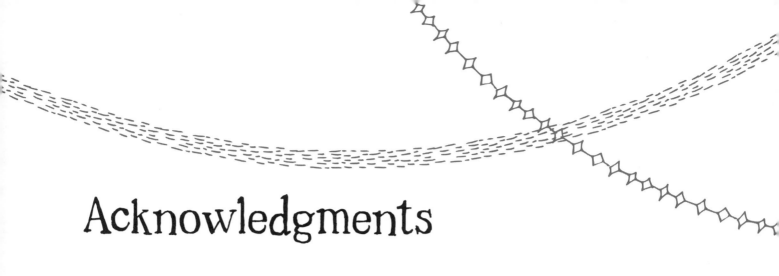

Acknowledgments

No book would be complete without specific mention of the special and talented people who helped shape it. I want to thank a multitude of people for helping to make this book possible.

I conceived the idea for this book while I was collecting data for my master's degree at Pacific Oaks College in Pasadena, California, in 1992. Some of the citations in this edition of *Celebrate!* refer to interviews I conducted for my unpublished master's thesis that year. My deepest thanks to the following educators, whose willingness to be interviewed and generosity with information helped to make this book what it is:

Cecelia Alvarado

ReGena Booze

Phyllis Brady

Sharon Cronin

Louise Derman-Sparks

Cory Gann

Cheryl Greer-Jarman

Eric J. Hoffman

Roberta Hunter

Katie Kissinger

Norma Quan Ong

Deborah Owens

Patricia G. Ramsey

B. J. Richards

Bill Sparks

Kim Sakamoto Steidl

Kay Taus

Stacey York

I am also grateful to Kendra PeloJoaquin, John Nimmo, Margie Carter, Deb Curtis, Louise Derman-Sparks, Fran Davidson, Karina Rojas, and Kristie Norwood for letting me interview you about your current thinking about and observations of holidays in practice in early learning programs. Your contributions helped frame my thinking for this revised edition. Thank you!

To the staff and families at Kidspace Child Care Center, thank you for your contributions to the first edition of this book. To my Epiphany Early Learning family, thank you for partnering with me every day and for never letting me stray from the values and vision we share.

Thank you to my editors, Ilene Rosen, editor of the first edition, and Jan Zita Grover, editor of the second edition. Thank you also to Mary Steiner Whelan, the former managing editor of Redleaf Press, for thinking this book was a good idea and encouraging me along the way.

Thank you to my family for never doubting that I could write this book and for being my biggest fans.

Gracias to my "second best" friend Linda Irene Jimenez, and to Louise Derman-Sparks: your mentoring and friendship will be forever precious to me.

Thank you to Jeff, my loving husband, for your unwavering excitement about this book and the revision. And to my children, Jonah and Jade—you were a twinkle in my eye when the first edition of *Celebrate!* was published in 1997, but I knew even then that I was writing it for you.

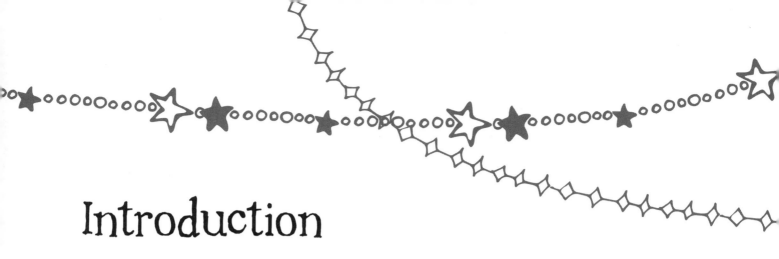

Introduction

INTRODUCTION TO THE SECOND EDITION

Almost twenty years have passed since I wrote *Celebrate!* Much has changed in early childhood education since then, and I was happy to be asked to update that first edition.

As you probably know from your own classroom, immigration has increased dramatically, early childhood education programs and home-based care are serving more diverse populations of children, and questions of how, when, and which holidays to celebrate have become more complex and controversial.

When I first wrote *Celebrate!*, I had just completed my graduate degree and my tenth year as an early childhood educator. Now I have thirty years in the field and am an administrator, and my range of experiences have added to my perspective on the ways holidays can be included in early learning classrooms. My goal here is to update you on methods for introducing familiar and unfamiliar holidays, backed by strategies for partnering with families and staff to develop agreed-upon practices.

I hope that you'll read the longer introduction to the 1997 edition of *Celebrate!*, which follows this one. Here, I'd like simply to point out some of the differences in how I now approach holidays in the program I administer.

The 1997 edition put information about planning holiday activities first. This time the nuts and bolts of classroom holiday activities come first. That's because possessing a good toolbox is invaluable to you, as a busy classroom teacher. This 2016 edition starts with a brief overview of what's changed demographically in U.S. early childhood programs and offers some ideas about why holiday practices haven't changed much in twenty years and what we need to commit to in order to effect change (chapter 1); offers proven ways to build successful holiday activities in your classroom (chapters 2 through 6); and describes proven processes for planning and implementing policy changes in your own program (chapters 7 through 12). Chapter 13 provides the perspectives of three classroom teachers who include holidays in their programs (private, nonprofit, secular; public, secular, Head Start; private, religious, sectarian).

The 2016 edition of *Celebrate!* ends with references that link you to the tremendous resources now available online. In 1997 I offered readers a bibliography of children's books on diversity, anti-bias education, and worldwide holidays; since then, much of the best information about these has migrated online. What you'll find here (appendix A) are my annotated list of reliable online resources for finding children's literature about holidays, along with updated resources for you on everything from how to plan individual holidays activities to how to talk about religion. In appendix B, I've included reproducible holiday policies, a sample questionnaire to compile family information about home holiday celebrations, a sample questionnaire about families' experiences with holidays in the classroom, and a sample Holiday Practices Improvement Plan that you can adapt to assess the strengths and weaknesses of your own holiday activities.

I hope you find this second edition of *Celebrate!* useful and supportive and that it helps you retain or regain the joy of discovering holidays with the children and families in your program.

INTRODUCTION TO THE FIRST EDITION

Why a Book about Holidays?

I have always loved holidays. When I was growing up, holidays were times of anticipation, festive feelings, warmth, and family togetherness.

As an early childhood educator, I carried my love of holidays into the classroom, wanting to re-create with the children what I had enjoyed with my family. It wasn't until I was teaching in the child care program at Pacific Oaks Children's School in Pasadena, California, and learning about anti-bias education that I began to feel uneasy about how I was approaching holidays in the classroom. As a staff, we put a lot of time and energy into researching holidays, but I began to doubt that children were gaining what I had hoped from the activities. They didn't always seem to be connecting to the underlying meaning of the holiday. In some cases, the holidays and their corresponding activities seemed too far removed from the children's own experiences to be meaningful. While my goal for many of the holiday activities was to help the children learn more about the people who celebrated them, I suspect that sometimes the children saw these people as "too different." They weren't able to see the parallels between themselves and the people whose holidays we were celebrating.

As I talked to other teachers and to teacher trainers, I discovered I wasn't the only one who had questions and concerns about holidays. This curriculum component had many of my colleagues and mentors feeling frustrated, confused, and overwhelmed.

My observations about holidays prompted me to research this topic for my master's thesis. I began by interviewing a multiethnic group of eighteen educators who are knowledgeable about both early childhood education and culturally relevant, anti-bias education. I asked them a series of questions about how holidays might be incorporated into an early childhood program using an anti-bias approach. The results of those interviews profoundly impacted my thinking about holidays and continue to affect my work in this area.

Over the last six years, I've presented many workshops on holidays and consulted with private and public early childhood programs as they made their own decisions about how to handle holidays. I have also struggled with this issue myself, as a director of a private, nonprofit child care program serving children aged two months through five years. These experiences continually remind me of the many different facets of holiday practices and the complexity of the challenges as well as the solutions.

About This Book

If you are a teacher, director, or supervisor in an early childhood program and are considering changing your approach to holidays, this book was written for you. It will also be useful to you if you are a teacher-trainer interested in helping teachers think about holidays in new ways. Holidays in the classroom are an area of much debate and struggle. Many teachers are grappling with this curriculum component. How to make holiday activities meaningful for children, how to relate them to their families, and how to implement activities accurately and respectfully are some of the many hurdles teachers face. Addressing diversity, avoiding stereotypes, handling the religious aspects of holidays, and meeting the needs of families who do not celebrate are others.

If you and I were sitting in a room and talking, instead of you reading these words on a page, I'd ask you what you hope to get from this book. Perhaps you are looking through it because you are uncomfortable with your current approach to holidays and are not sure how to change it. Possibly your program or classroom presently has a policy of not celebrating holidays because of the difficulty in doing them well, and you would prefer to find ways to include holidays using a more effective approach. Or maybe you are reading this book to find ideas for celebrating specific holidays, like Kwanzaa.

While you will find ideas in these pages for celebrating holidays, you should know that this is not a holiday activity book. Instead, this book attempts to create a framework of things to consider about how to create holiday activities that are enjoyable for children, and are also in tune with the anti-bias approach that includes being meaningful, culturally appropriate, and inclusive. It is meant to be a guide as you answer your own questions about how to handle holidays in your setting.

How to Use This Book

Throughout this book, you will find ideas and suggestions about working with families, which is a critical part of planning and implementing an inclusive, sensitive holiday program. For ease of reading, the book will generally refer to parents and guardians or families when referring to any adults who care for and care about a child in your program, including grandparents, partners or companions, legal guardians, and other important adults in children's lives.

This book is organized in sequential fashion to help you go about the process of reflecting on and changing your approach to holidays. You might find it useful to start at the beginning and read each chapter in order. If you don't plan to read the entire book from start to finish, and you are the kind of person who likes to jump into action, start with the second section. It will refer you to other places in the book to find the information you need as you go along. On the other hand, if you prefer to get all the information before you act, you might like to start with the third section. The first section includes important information that you should read before you actually implement changes in your program, but it doesn't have to be read before the other sections of the book.

A Message to You, the Reader

As you work through this book and through your own efforts to provide a more effective holiday curriculum, it may help you to think of the process as a journey, one that will continue for a long time to come. I welcome you on that journey.

For me, it has been somewhat like going through an old trunk of my grandmother's that I found in the attic. As I pulled off the top layer of clothes and memoirs, I felt overwhelmed with feelings and responsibilities. I worked through those issues and then dug deeper, only to find more surprises and challenges. The process continued with intermittent joy, sadness, regret, and relief. I finally got to the bottom of the trunk, but I often revisit the items that I found buried underneath one another.

I suspect that you too will make some mistakes on your journey, and you will have some tremendous successes. This is hard work. Holidays have been a focal point of early childhood curriculum for many years, and old habits are hard to break. And since holidays can be very personal and emotional, you will probably encounter some strong emotions and possibly some resistance as you go forward on your journey. Don't give up! Change may be slow, but that's okay. Take baby steps. Every small move forward is an accomplishment. As you proceed through your journey, remember: the thought and effort you put in will make you a more effective teacher and create a more responsive environment for your children.

I also want you, the reader, to know that I am a European American woman. I identify strongly with my Italian American heritage. I grew up on the East

Coast and have spent the last eleven years on the West Coast. Like any writer, my identity and my life experiences have shaped what I have written on these pages.

My intent in this book is to offer you guideposts for your journey, not to tell you exactly how to handle holidays. I hope that you'll find this information useful as you make your own decisions about how to approach holidays in your program. Good luck!

PART ONE

....

Rethinking Holidays in the Classroom

CHAPTER 1

The Holiday Question Has Become More Complex

Almost twenty years have passed since I wrote the first edition of *Celebrate!* Most of the challenges teachers and programs faced then still present challenges today. Holidays continue to be deeply meaningful for people, and programs are still looking for answers to the holiday question: "How do we handle holidays in a meaningful way—one that is not focused on commercialism, that reflects the diversity of our families and community, and that doesn't offend anyone?" If you work in a city or suburb where there is quite a bit of diversity, you may have seen that it has become increasingly difficult to answer this holiday question and meet the sometimes seemingly conflicting needs of supervisors, teachers, parents or guardians, and children.

THE UNITED STATES HAS CHANGED

In my own experience as a director of a child care program in Seattle, which is part of King County in Washington State, I have seen tremendous changes in the population of children and families in programs. These changes have led to more complexities. I'll describe these changes as just one example of what you too may be dealing with in your community.

Since 1997, when the first edition of this book was published, King County has grown tremendously. For example, from 2000 to 2012, King County gained 220,000 persons, which for us is an 11 percent population growth. More than half of that recent growth is of immigrants from all parts of Asia, Latin American, Eastern Europe, and Africa. Further, the number of individuals who speak languages other than English has vastly increased. In the year 2000, 299,600 individuals in King County spoke languages other than English. By the year 2011, 462,200 spoke languages other than English; the majority of these spoke Spanish, Chinese, Vietnamese, Somali and Amharic, Tagalog, and Korean (King County Office of Performance, Strategy, and Budget 2013).

The population in my neck of the woods reflects the overall population growth in the United States. The country as a whole has seen an explosion in immigration. For example, in 2014 approximately 42.4 million immigrants were living in the United States. This is 13.3 percent of the country's 318.9 million residents. If you add the U.S.-born children of these immigrants, approximately 81 million people, or one quarter of the U.S. population, are either first- or second-generation residents (Migration Policy Institute 2016).

As a result of these changes in population, the holiday question has become even more complex, bringing new urgency to such questions as "How do we include holidays from the diversity of our families in a way that is not inaccurate or stereotypical, especially if we aren't familiar with these holidays ourselves?" and "Is it okay to still celebrate Halloween, Christmas, Thanksgiving, Easter, and other dominant-culture holidays?" With the increasing number of religions among new residents of Seattle and other U.S. cities, more families in your and my programs may have questions about the underlying meanings of the holidays we've been celebrating for years in our classrooms.

Here is one example. A center I know serves an increasingly diverse community of families, of whom about 25 percent are Latino, 25 percent are European American, 40 percent are Asian (Vietnamese, Chinese, and Korean), along with a smaller and newer group of Somali families. As Muslims, these Somali families do not participate in any Christian celebrations. The teachers in this program are primarily Latina, and they try to be considerate and respectful of the Somali families by notifying them when holiday activities are planned so they can keep their children at home if they are uncomfortable with the activities.

This year the teachers gave some careful thought to their holiday practices and decided that, because they themselves are a part of the program community, they would like to share a holiday that is very important to them with the children and families in their program: Día de los Muertos (Day of the Dead), a most important holiday that honors and remembers their ancestors. In the words of their director, "We wouldn't be here if it weren't for our ancestors." The teachers were overjoyed to bring in elements of their beloved holiday to share with the children and families in the program. As the Day of the Dead activities were introduced and the altar/table was set up with sugar skulls and photos of loved ones who had departed, several conversations ensued. First, some of the families who are Somali and practicing Muslims were unsure about the holiday and had to consider whether or not to keep their children home during the activities. The European American families who didn't celebrate the holiday were excited and eager for their children to learn a bit about the culture of Mexicans and other Latinos, and they were very comfortable with their children participating in the activities. Some of the Latino families who have children in the program, however, were not comfortable with the activities because they seemed too much like Halloween, which for them was equivalent to devil worship and something they did not want their children exposed to. A new family had just arrived and told the director that they were practicing members of a Christian religion that forbade celebrations. The director was unsure how all of these conflicting perspectives were going to play out, but she was committed to making sure the family received notice before planned activities so the parents could decide if their children could participate.

It's not only the movement of people seeking better lives and better jobs that has altered the populations of cities, suburbs, and the early learning programs serving them. Many early childhood educators have come to embrace and celebrate this increasing diversity and are striving to create programs rich in anti-bias practices backed by their strong belief that everyone is enriched by programs that celebrate the practices and beliefs of their entire community. However, since the first edition of *Celebrate!* was published, we've seen an increase in polarization. More programs now are choosing a no-holiday approach in the hope that this practice will remove the contentious feelings and perspectives surrounding the issue of holidays in the classroom. At the same time, many early learning programs and elementary schools are finding that avoiding holidays fuels the controversy too: many people who celebrate dominant-culture holidays like Halloween, Thanksgiving, and Christmas are furious that they can longer celebrate these "American" holidays in classrooms.

My twenty-year perspective

I have come to believe that the main reason holidays have always been difficult for early childhood programs and the directors, teachers, and parents in them and perhaps why they are even more contentious now is that we tend not to want to deal with the deeper issues underlying holidays. These require respect, listening, humility, and a commitment to working together until everyone's needs are met and everyone is included.

So while early learning programs look and aspire to function more expansively than they did twenty years ago, when *Celebrate!* was first published, programs still struggle with the original holiday question, and now have many more questions and complexities added to the mix. That, along with an avoidance of the deeper, underlying beliefs that can spur conflict, has put us in a position where most programs have not changed much in the ways we handle holidays. It's time to look at what's underneath. It's time to look at why we still haven't solved this and why more and more programs lean toward no holiday celebrations.

COMPLEXITIES AND DIFFERING PERSPECTIVES

Because of our diverse histories, faiths, and cultures, the same holiday can have various meanings to people. If you put thirty people who celebrate a particular holiday in a room, though you will find some commonalities in beliefs and practice, you will also see many, many different ways of celebrating. One of the most important lessons to keep in mind as you embark on a new way of handling holidays in your program is that there are many differing perspectives and beliefs about every single holiday.

Some perspectives are religious

The increased diversity in the United States has brought people with different religious beliefs and practices into close contact. While the majority of Americans identify themselves as Christians, many living in this country and enrolled in our programs practice other religions, including Judaism, Buddhism, Islam, and Hinduism. People of different faiths and spiritual beliefs often possess strong opinions about the religious aspects of holidays.

For example, some see Halloween as a rite of childhood, an opportunity for children to do what they love—dress up, flirt with elements of darkness, become frightened, and eat candy! Others, however, view Halloween as devil worship, a practice against their own beliefs, and they don't feel comfortable participating in the holiday or allowing their children to participate in trick-or-treating, carving or displaying pumpkins, or wearing costumes on or near this day.

Here's another example. Some people see Hanukkah as a cultural celebration, one that reminds those who are Jewish of their history and heritage. Others view it as an emphatically religious celebration that includes the miracle of lantern oil that lasted for eight nights during the rededication of the second temple.

Some people see evergreen trees in school lobbies in December as symbols of winter, while others see them as symbols of the Christian holiday Christmas. For Christians, the Christmas season can be a joyous time for connecting with others and celebrating shared religious beliefs. Christmas is widely celebrated in the United States as a national holiday; businesses, schools, banks, government agencies, and most retail stores are closed. For many non-Christians, popular emphasis on this day can feel ostracizing.

Many Chinese Americans view Chinese New Year as a purely cultural event celebrating and evoking a prosperous new year. From their perspective, because the holiday does not arise from any religion or religious purpose, it is secular, not religious. For others, however, the spiritual means used by some to help ensure a good year make it religious. Chinese New Year is often celebrated with firecrackers, lanterns, torches, and bonfires to chase away evil spirits with light and noise. Many Chinese and Chinese American families hang a kitchen god in their kitchens who is believed to return to heaven just before Chinese New Year to report on their household over the past year to the Jade Emperor.

Some perspectives are cultural

Other holidays are secular but no less controversial. For most American families, Thanksgiving is a happy, warm holiday about togetherness and giving thanks for food and other blessings. The holiday also celebrates their shared perspective on history, a story about goodwill and friendship. However, to others, especially those who are American Indian, Thanksgiving can be a reminder of centuries of unfairness and hurt, a holiday that marks the beginning of a devastating time in their history when promises were broken, possessions were stolen, and families were separated and killed.

Similarly, many Americans view Columbus Day as an opportunity to remember Columbus as a brave explorer whose daring, perseverance, and navigational skill led to the "discovery" of America. Others believe it is important to tell the story of how Christopher Columbus ushered in centuries of death and oppression for those who lived on this continent before his arrival. As a result, some believe that Columbus Day is an important historical event that should be commemorated every year and others feel strongly otherwise.

Many see Valentine's Day as the perfect holiday for preschoolers, an opportunity to talk about love and friendship and to practice telling others how you feel about them by writing valentines and practicing literacy and writing skills to boot! For others, however, Valentine's Day has become an adult holiday taken over by Hallmark and has no place in an early learning classroom.

Some families don't celebrate holidays at all

Here's yet another perspective: many people living in the United States don't celebrate holidays at all. Our society's emphasis on holidays, particularly on those that fall between October and January, can cause difficulties for some families and their children in your programs.

MULTIPLE PERSPECTIVES PROVIDE AN OPPORTUNITY TO COME TOGETHER

The most important lesson here is that it doesn't matter whose perspective seems right. What should really matter to us as educators is that we learn the differing perspectives among families and staff so we know where to begin. Because regardless of our intentions or of what we mean to portray or communicate, if even one family sees it differently than we do and feels uncomfortable, we must pause and commit ourselves to a conversation. We need to uncover what underlies that discomfort in order to move forward so that all families feel comfortable with our practices. This is a tremendous opportunity for learning and coming together.

The differing perspectives on holidays among the staff and families in your program will affect your activities and conversations about holidays. Whether your group is diverse or relatively homogeneous, there will be vast differences in the ways they celebrate and how they view the same holidays. Keeping this in mind will be essential to moving forward with holidays in your program.

Most programs' holiday practices haven't changed much

If a visitor entered your classroom when you and the children were involved in a holiday activity or discussion, what would they see and feel? Would they see children connected by feelings of warmth and community, and being seen for what is important to their families? Would they learn a little bit about the underlying meaning of the holiday? Would they see children involved in activities that they were comfortable with? Could they tell that the activities reflected the home lives of the children in the classroom?

Perhaps they would not. In many programs across the country, holidays are not treated with the planning, preparation, and sensitivity they require. Instead, teachers with very good intentions use them as a primary method for organizing the year's curriculum or as a way to teach culture, without realizing the negative impact that results when holidays are used in this way.

In talking with colleagues around the country while revising *Celebrate!* I learned that the same traps I identified twenty years ago still challenge many early childhood educators today. Here's a brief summary of those traps and why they don't work.

TRAP #1: HOLIDAYS BY HABIT

Many early childhood educators pride themselves on curriculum boxes or files of proven activities that they use each year. We may rely on these boxes, returning to them time and time again to bring out familiar activities that worked with groups in past years. This is sometimes the case with holidays in early childhood programs. When October comes around, the Halloween box may come down off the shelf and then the Thanksgiving box in November, the "winter" box in December, and so on. However, with each new group of children and with each new year comes an opportunity to reevaluate what we've done in the past, to get to know the children in our classroom and design curriculum with them in mind, and to use new techniques in addition to our proven ideas to move forward.

I recently received a phone call from a colleague I hadn't seen in a while. She was cleaning out her storage areas. She had led a program for preschoolers for many years and had since closed her doors. Though she was very attached to the materials she had been storing, which I would describe as theme boxes, she just didn't have the space for them anymore, and she really wanted another program to take advantage of them. It was very powerful to go to her home and watch her sort through box upon box and show me her North Pole box, rain forest box, and winter holiday box, along with countless others. With each lid she opened, she sighed and said, "Oh, I love this one. This is such a rich unit." And I graciously accepted any of these wonderful materials she wanted to give to my program and supported her when she told me which ones she wasn't quite ready to give up yet. I was moved by the heart and care and intention and resources she had put into each box.

As I drove these materials back to my program that afternoon, I reflected on how this colleague is like many others I know. She worked so hard to put together an expensive collection of units based on themes that had worked for her in the past, and she was quite invested in them, and for good reason! But I knew that these units, as packaged, would not get used as-is in my program. Instead, they would be carefully organized, stored, and then pulled out, maybe as a unit but more likely one by one as a material or set of materials, in response to children's current interests and development themes. We use what we know about the children in our program, our observations of their investigations, and current play themes in our classrooms to determine what to offer them next. Just pulling a box off a shelf doesn't work for us anymore.

This is true of holiday activities too. We can't assume that the children and families in our program this year will celebrate the same holidays that children did last year, or that all families will be comfortable with our holiday activities from last year. It takes a careful reevaluation each year as well as ongoing communication with families to determine what holidays will be shared or celebrated.

TRAP #2: USING HOLIDAYS TO TEACH ABOUT CULTURE, INCLUDING THE TOURIST TRAP

Early childhood educators know the value of celebrating cultural diversity in the classroom, so we seek out available resources for ideas about how to do that. Much of what we find is strategies that use holidays to teach culture and celebrate diversity.

The problem with this approach arises when holidays become the main or sole avenue for teaching about cultural diversity. We end up trivializing the culture and inadvertently make cultural groups seem so different, so exotic, that we cannot identify with them at all. Culture is not easily taught through simple activities that focus on only special and unique times of the year. People learn about their own culture starting at birth, through daily life. They learn about others' lives over time by getting to know the people of that culture and how they live their daily lives. Because holidays are special times during the year when business-as-usual comes to a halt, children can't learn about the usual, everyday routines of another cultural group by only learning about their holidays.

Louise Derman-Sparks and Julie Olsen Edwards, in their book *Anti-Bias Education for Young Children and Ourselves* (2010), use the term *the tourist approach* to describe attempts to teach about a culture through holidays, because children only visit a culture briefly, perhaps participate in a few isolated activities, as they might do on vacation in another country, then return home to regular classroom life. Often images of the people whose holiday the class celebrates are absent from the classroom for the rest of the year, until that same holiday rolls around again.

We see this in attempts to teach preschoolers about people who are Mexican by celebrating Cinco de Mayo (Fifth of May). This is a holiday that celebrates Mexico's liberation from French rule. This battle victory inspired many people fighting for Mexican independence, but it was not the most important battle in those many years of struggle. Nevertheless, some people in Mexico and the United States celebrate this holiday to commemorate Mexico's victory.

But in early childhood programs, Cinco de Mayo is often used as an opportunity to teach children about people who are Mexican and Mexican American. Some common activities used to celebrate this holiday include making a piñata; making tortillas; eating burritos for lunch; using serapes, sombreros, and Mexican cooking utensils in the dramatic play area; counting in Spanish; and learning a Mexican hat dance. The underlying reason for the holiday is not taught.

Thus the holiday's meaning, as well as an understanding of the diversity of Mexican and Mexican American people, is lost in these celebrations. The activities teach nothing about the daily lives of Mexican people and how they go about working, learning, playing, or loving their families. Such activities neglect the many connections and similarities between Mexican and Mexican American children and American children of other ethnic backgrounds, and instead focus solely on differences.

What children may learn by participating only in these activities is that all Mexican and Mexican American people celebrate Cinco de Mayo (which is not true), that all Mexican and Mexican American people wear serapes and sombreros (also not true), and that the important things about Mexicans and Mexican Americans is that they celebrate Cinco de Mayo, eat burritos, and eat candy that comes from piñatas (clearly not true).

In addition, this approach to learning about Cinco de Mayo overlooks the vast differences among the lives of people who live in different parts of Mexico and the differences between Mexicans living in Mexico and Mexican Americans living in the United States. These prevalent Cinco de Mayo activities can be hurtful and confusing to Mexican and Mexican American children, as well as to their classmates, if their lives don't match the holiday descriptions of "what Mexicans do."

This tourist approach occurs while teaching/celebrating other holidays as well. Thanksgiving is used as a time to teach about American Indians;

Kwanzaa is used to teach children about African Americans; and Ramadan is sometimes used to teach about Muslims around the world. But using holidays to anchor learning about different cultures runs the risk of trivializing a cultural group by implying that the most important thing about it is a holiday; promoting misinformation (sometimes historical) about a cultural group by disconnecting the meaning of the holiday from the context of current daily life; and promoting views of "exotic" people who don't do daily life activities but rather sing, dance, and eat special foods. Such approaches overemphasize the differences between people rather than demonstrating the ways in which we are both similar to and different from one another.

TRAP #3: CHANGING THE NAME BUT DOING THE SAME THING

One of the common strategies used in early education to avoid conflict and concern about holidays is to keep most of the activities that teachers and families love and just call them something different. For example, it's now common to refer to Halloween parties and activities as Harvest Festivals, at which, on October 31, children don costumes, trick-or-treat, carve jack-o'-lanterns, and guess the amount of candy corn in the jar. But families who are uncomfortable with Halloween activities are still going to be uncomfortable with them even though they've been renamed a Harvest Festival.

Similarly, in many programs a December gathering of children and families at which they make ornaments and sing "Rudolf the Red-Nosed Reindeer" and "Frosty the Snowman" is now called a Winter Celebration. Often there is an attempt to add diversity by including the song "I Have a Little Dreidel," but one song about Hanukkah among four or five others that may not say but invoke the word *Christmas* still looks and sounds like a Christmas performance to many. Parents who don't celebrate Christmas see right through this attempt to be more multicultural during the winter holidays.

Changing the name but not the game is a very, very common practice, but it doesn't reflect the thinking and planning needed to create holiday experiences in which everyone can truly participate. Simply changing the name but continuing the same activities isn't real change and isn't likely to meet the needs of all of your children and families.

TRAP #4: EXCLUDING CHILDREN WHOSE FAMILIES' BELIEFS PREVENT THEM FROM PARTICIPATING

As an early childhood educator for the last thirty years, I've learned one fundamental fact about teachers: you are doing your absolutely best work with the resources, education, and support available to you. None of us means to offend, upset, or exclude anyone. We continue to learn, grow, and seek support and direction to do the very best job we can.

One of the strategies we sometimes use with the best of intentions when we have a family whose religious or cultural practice precludes their child from participating in holiday activities is to promise to give them ample notice if they choose to keep their child home on a holiday activity day. Or we may choose to respect parents' or guardians' wishes that their child not sing in the holiday pageant by "inviting" that child to visit another classroom while all of their friends are practicing for the big show.

At first glance, these might seem like perfect solutions. After all, aren't we listening to and respecting the wishes of families and protecting their children from having to choose between their families' cultural or religious beliefs and what the other children are doing? However, this approach results in families who must take time off from work to stay home with their children and children who feel ostracized and embarrassed when they are separated and excluded from their classmates.

In several of my holiday workshops, I've listened to Jewish adults who have recounted painful memories of such exclusions in classrooms where the air was abuzz with Christmas. They recalled the Christmas decorations on bulletin boards, the Christmas tree in the corner of the room, the invitations to participate in making Christmas ornaments or painting Christmas wrapping paper. Because they didn't celebrate Christmas, they were instead invited to a small table in the corner of the room, where they could decorate a Star of David with blue and white paint, or they were sent to another classroom of children they didn't know, where they sat quietly at a table while that class participated in its usual non-holiday activities, until the Jewish children could return to their now Christmas activity–free classroom and rejoin their peers.

While these adults spoke of these experiences, they often cried or turned the embarrassment and isolation they felt into anger that they had been made to feel like their families' beliefs were wrong and that they were less important than the children who celebrated Christmas.

Is this what we want for the children and families we serve? Yet it continues to happen in many programs to children from many backgrounds.

TRAP #5: JUST SAYING NO

Because of these many difficulties, it is becoming more and more common today for early childhood directors and program supervisors to put a stop to all holiday activities. It's not hard to understand why. A program may include a myriad of families with seemingly opposing positions, and staff may feel overwhelmed and believe that attempts to meet everyone's needs are futile.

Imagine a program, just like many others in the United States, where several different strongly held beliefs operate simultaneously. In this program, you may have teachers who are eager to share their personal holiday traditions with the children, and parents who are concerned about that because of the position of power teachers hold. The parents worry that their children will learn that the "right" holidays to celebrate, and sometimes the "right" religion to practice, are those of the classroom teachers instead of the families' own. In another classroom down the hall, you might have a couple of teachers who are upset that the story of Christmas and the associated activities in classrooms have been reduced to evergreen trees and Santa, when the essence of Christmas as they know it and live it is about the birth of baby Jesus. Across the hall, you might find teachers who are Jewish and have sad memories of having been banished to another classroom when Christmas activities were offered during their childhoods. And at the other end of the hall, you might have teachers who don't want to recognize Christmas or any other dominant-culture holiday because they believe that Hallmark has taken over most major holidays to promote commercialism. The children in this classroom who celebrate Christmas at home may wonder why their teachers talk about Solstice but not Christmas. You might also have a teacher who sees the value of introducing children to every holiday and so packs the curriculum from October through January with activities from all cultures, some of which are practiced by families in the program but others which are not. Her coteacher might have heard at a conference that if she is committed to an anti-bias approach, she shouldn't celebrate *any* holidays, so she acknowledges only the changes in the seasons and avoids even saying the words *Halloween*, *Thanksgiving*, *Hanukkah*, or *Christmas*.

You might have in the same classroom a child whose Jewish parent wants to come in and share the cultural aspects of Hanukkah with the children and a Christian parent who believes that Hanukkah is a religious holiday and that because she can't share the religious story of Christmas, the story of Hanukkah should not be shared either. In that same classroom, you might also have parents whose religion or cultural values preclude their children from participating in any holiday activities at school, and other parents who do celebrate and feel that their children are being deprived of their right to holiday activities because a few other families don't celebrate. Down the hall, you might find parents who are outraged that children can't dress up for Halloween, and other parents who won't allow their children to come to school if Halloween activities are offered, because the holiday goes against their religious values.

Is it any wonder, then, that many early childhood educators and programs have decided to leave holidays behind, hoping that doing so will eliminate the conflict and strife that now often accompany classroom holiday activities?

But this is not the answer either. Eliminating holidays deprives everyone, most particularly children, of opportunities to see and be seen, and to learn and grow from one another's practices and values.

RETHINKING HOLIDAYS IN THE CLASSROOM

Holidays in early childhood classrooms often mean special food and art activities. Because of concerns about how to handle the religious aspects of holidays or fear of offending someone who doesn't subscribe to a particular holiday, teachers and children rarely talk about religion. However, many holidays are based on religious stories, and for families who celebrate holidays at home, the stories behind them and the rituals they include often have profound meanings, bringing together experiences that touch the cores of their lives, including family, friends, values, and religion or spirituality. Before you can find new answers for handling holidays, you may need to step back and look at what holidays are and why they can be so significant, so culturally and spiritually important for the people who celebrate them.

Think about your own experiences with holidays. Is there one that is particularly special to you as an adult, one that you really enjoy celebrating? Consider for a moment why that holiday is important to you. What about it is so special? What feelings does it bring up for you? The answers to these questions may reveal some of your values and the underlying meaning of this holiday for you.

Not all adults enjoy or participate in holidays. But those who do often name similar values, similar reasons for celebrating: values such as love, connectedness, joy, sense of wonder, thankfulness, remembering ancestors, as well as independence and standing up for what you believe in. Let's take a closer look at some of the common values or reasons for celebrating that many adults hold.

Relating to family and friends

Almost without fail, when adults share what they love the most about a particular holiday, one of the answers is about being with family and friends. It's about getting together with the people you love, whether they are related by blood or are part of your chosen family. Sometimes this can be a group of friends, if you are far from the family members you grew up with and yearn to be with during this special time. During these gatherings, family members share memories and re-create special family recipes and traditions that connect them to their childhoods and culture. In the case of chosen friends, people often bring something to the holiday that they shared in their childhood, or as a group they create new recipes and traditions.

Connecting to culture

Many holiday traditions are closely tied to the cultures that our parents and grandparents came from. Participating in cultural traditions, like gathering around the piano to sing songs that have been passed down or making traditional recipes the way Grandma did, helps people feel closer to their culture and to their ancestors. Holidays provide an opportunity to feel a part of something larger than ourselves. They also provide opportunities for us to pass along the same cultural traditions and values to a new generation.

Anticipating and making magic

Many holidays contain elements of magic. The rituals of preparing for these holidays—cooking, decorating, shopping, participating in traditional activities, even cleaning—may conjure up wonderful feelings of warmth, excitement, and anticipation. These feelings often begin before the holiday arrives and may linger long after. Adults who recall the magic of waking up on Christmas morning to see presents under the tree, baking with a beloved aunt or grandmother, or searching for the afikomen at the end of a Seder, often yearn to reexperience those same feelings in their adult lives by reliving or creating new traditions that instill those feelings of magic. Parents and guardians are often eager to offer the same experiences with the same feelings of magic to their children through the same or similar traditions.

Experiencing the rhythms of life

For many of us, the pressure of busy, fast-paced lives creates a whirlwind, a demanding day-to-day existence. In this whirlwind, we sometimes forget who we are, and we search for ways to make meaning or sense out of our lives. Holidays that come around at the same time each year can help remind us of who we are and what is important to us. They also remind us of the cyclical nature of the seasons and the ever-present cycle of birth and death. Participating in familiar, cyclical traditions each year can bring a sense of security and predictability to our ever-changing world and busy lives.

Living our spirituality and religion

Spirituality plays a large role in holidays for many of us. The vast majority of holidays are built on religious stories or religious beliefs. Going to our place of worship, singing special songs, recounting historical and/or religious stories, and eating significant foods can all reinforce our beliefs about the world. For many, if the religious story is left out of a discussion about holidays, there is little left. For others, the religious part of the story is less important and some of the other underlying values, such as love, joy, magic, giving, thankfulness, and fighting for fairness, take center stage.

Creating identity

Holidays serve the needs of the individuals and groups who celebrate them. They teach the values of a particular group and a particular version of history and often reinforce relationships to a chosen deity. Holidays and their rituals serve as reminders to adults and teach young people what the group considers important. Knowing what holidays mean to you personally is an essential first step, because this will be a lens through which you see and experience all holiday activities, discussions, and decision making.

WHY CELEBRATE HOLIDAYS IN THE CLASSROOM?

By now you might be wondering what the alternatives are to the current, and less than successful, approaches to holidays that I have mentioned. You may even be thinking that the problems with holidays are too complex to solve in your program.

The answer lies in the choices you make as an early childhood teacher or administrator. Below you'll find my choices and those of the program I administer. I offer them to you not as a template but as how one administrator, one staff, and one group of families have chosen to bring celebrations into young children's classrooms.

We include all families

Leaving holidays out of children's classroom experiences can have negative consequences, especially for those children whose holidays are not typically reflected in the dominant culture. If you are a child (or adult) whose holidays are not typically reflected in stores, in television programming, on holiday cards, in decorations, and so on, knowing that your holiday is also omitted by your early childhood program can be very painful (Sharon Cronin, interview with author, April 1992). Excluding holidays from your program leaves out important parts of many families' lives.

We teach that different beliefs enrich all of our lives and community

It is extremely beneficial for children to hear the important adults in their lives talk about the ways that people are alike and different from one another. This is one of the basic tenets of the anti-bias approach to education and an important foundation for children to acquire before they enter elementary school and the increasingly diverse world beyond it.

One of the biggest gifts we can give children is learning to find joy in human differences as well as to see connections between themselves and others. Discussions about holidays in our community provide another opportunity to do just that. Children can learn that many of us celebrate and that many of us celebrate the same holidays in different ways. They can also learn that their classmates may not celebrate what they do, but they can come to understand that other people's celebrations are just as important, just as worthy as their own. When teachers model genuine interest in and respect for families' home practices, children learn the value of different practices and beliefs in enriching community.

In my program, families are invited to come in at any time of the year and share a recipe, a story, a photo, a song, or an activity about a holiday that is important in their home. During fall and winter holiday time, we might have one family coming in each week to share with us. One week we might have a parent come in and talk about Diwali and the importance of light in that celebration. The next week, a parent could come in and give a synopsis of the Hanukkah story and the significance of the oil in the lanterns lasting for eight days. Then the parent of a child who celebrates Christmas might come in and talk about how their family celebrates by putting lights on the tree and on the house and singing songs about baby Jesus. The teachers in the classroom would continually make connections between the holidays that are important to families in the classroom: "Dipali celebrates Diwali at home, where her family lights many different kinds of candles and lights, and Hazel celebrates Hanukkah and lights a menorah for eight days, and Luke decorates his Christmas tree with lots of different lights. All of you are celebrating, and all of you have lights in this holiday you love, but your holidays are not the same. You are both the same and different!"

We validate and reflect important parts of families' lives

Holiday discussions and activities can be one more way that teachers help children feel validated for who they are and what they do at home with their families. Whether or not children see themselves reflected in their environment is one of the ways they get messages about their value and worth. By having families come in and share information about their special celebrations, their children learn that who they are and what is important to their family is valued by the teachers and others in their school community. This can be especially valuable when the holiday being celebrated is a non-dominant-culture holiday and the children rarely see it reflected or hear it talked about beyond their own homes.

Here is an example of the power of including holidays that reflect the family experiences of those enrolled. A preschool program in Southern California has a diverse group of children and families from different backgrounds. One year the teacher, ReGena, became aware that one of the families was Persian (Iranian). When the mother came in the first day of school to drop off her children, ReGena approached her and asked if her family celebrated Nowruz (Iranian New Year). The mother instantly grabbed ReGena's arm and exclaimed, "Oh, I will like it here! No one has ever asked me that before!" The mother's surprise and delight at ReGena's knowledge about her culture and the idea of including this holiday in her child's program helped her to feel connected, safe, and comfortable in the school environment. Later ReGena went to her classroom library, pulled out a couple of books that included Nowruz and other Iranian holidays, and asked the mother if the information accurately reflected what her family believed and practiced. When the holiday arrived in March, the mother came in and introduced some relevant activities to the children. The familiar holiday activities, along with other culturally relevant discussions and materials that ReGena included in the program, affected her and the child's comfort and identification with the classroom. Because the interactions, environment, and activities were culturally relevant, this child and her family thrived in the program (ReGena Booze, interview with author, April 1992).

Even if the holidays a family celebrates are the traditional dominant-culture holidays that show up in stores, books, television shows, and decorations, it is still important and valuable to reflect and validate how and what is celebrated in children's homes. For example, many children in the United States celebrate Christmas and see Christmas reflected everywhere from October to December, but children yearn for the important adults in their lives to understand what it means in *their* families and in *their* homes to be getting ready for Christmas: what it smells like, who is going to be there, what presents were received, and other traditions. All children deserve and yearn to be seen in this way.

We strengthen school-family and parent-teacher partnerships

Sometimes inviting a family to share one of its most treasured home traditions with children in the classroom provides an opportunity for more than just holiday sharing: it may also open a door to trust, respect, and connection, and these lead to deeper partnerships between parents and teachers.

This is exactly what happened in my program recently. One of the preschool teachers was trying unsuccessfully to connect with the parents of one of the children in her class. Both parents worked, and they dropped their child off early and buzzed out the door to get to work, then swooped back in at the end of their busy day to reunite with their daughter and head home for dinner.

After reading the family's holiday questionnaire and learning that they celebrated Diwali at home, the teacher asked the parents if they would be willing to share some of their tradition with the class. A new partnership was born. The parents were delighted to have been asked, and several meetings, e-mail exchanges, and conversations occurred while preparations were made for them to visit the classroom.

When the actual day came, both parents spent an hour in the classroom sharing two traditional dishes, some stories, and a variety of candles and other lights to emphasize the theme of light in this holiday. Their child beamed during their visit, and in the days following, the little girl seemed to feel more connected to her peers in the classroom. So did her parents. This was the spark that eventually led to a deeper and more intentional relationship and partnership between the parents and the teacher. That invitation to the family to come in and share their treasured and special family tradition and subsequent conversations and planning between family and teacher built trust and opened the door to more dialogue and sharing. The family's daughter and all of the other children in the classroom benefited.

We commit ourselves to thoughtful dialogue between staff and families

For me, one of the greatest benefits of committing to a meaningful, inclusive approach to holidays is the dialogue that must take place within the staff and between the staff and families to create a policy and practices that work. In the early childhood field—or perhaps it's just with humans in general—we don't like conflict. We shy away from hard conversations where there are lots of emotions, and we often do whatever we can to gloss over real issues so we can move on and can get past the discomfort. One thing I'm absolutely certain of is that we cannot create approaches to holidays that work for everyone in our programs unless we open our hearts and our minds and commit to discovering the values, opinions, beliefs, and convictions that can only be uncovered and understood through dialogue.

HOW WE BEGIN THE DIALOGUE

In my program, when new families enroll, we require them to attend a new-family orientation where we begin to get to know one another. We ask the families to think of a favorite early memory from their childhood, one that stands out from the rest, one that is positive. When we ask everyone to share the "why" that goes along with this memory—why it is one of their favorite memories—we hear things like "I got up in the morning, hopped on my bike, rode around the neighborhood, met with friends, and I didn't come home until supper," or "I used to swing with my friend Merilee on the rope swing in my backyard and sing songs and do routines."

When families share, we pull out the values we hear in their stories, values like connection to the outdoors, being with friends and family, feeling independent, long stretches of uninterrupted time. This is the first time we ask families to share something about themselves with us, but it's definitely not the last. A few weeks after orientation, families attend our curriculum night, when instead of just telling families exactly what is going to happen for their children in the toddler or preschool room this year, we again ask families to share with us.

This year we asked families to recall an early memory of school and what feelings they had about it. We also asked them to share their thoughts on school readiness and the values they hold about school in their family. We asked questions like "Do you view preschool primarily as an opportunity for open-ended play or as an opportunity to gain school readiness skills?" The point here is that the moment families enter our program, we crave to be in a relationship with them. We share of ourselves and earn the trust of families so they feel comfortable sharing with us.

Like many early childhood educators, I ask families to fill out copious forms and other pieces of paper when their children enroll. One of these is a holiday questionnaire in which I ask families to share what they celebrate at home, how they celebrate, and how they'd feel about their children learning about other holidays, including the religious stories in other holidays (see Sample Family Questionnaire about Holidays in appendix B, page 169). We review these questionnaires as soon as they are turned in, but we also review them periodically throughout the year. If families indicate that they'd be concerned about their children learning about Jewish holidays or Muslim holidays, for example, then we ask for a meeting with them, an opportunity to learn more. Our goal as educators when we meet with the family is to truly listen, to do our best to ask open-ended questions, and to avoid mentally preparing our objection or counterargument before the parent even finishes explaining. Then we share what we've typically done in the past, how we typically talk about a particular holiday or the religious story within that holiday, and we ask more questions: "How would this land for you? What would make you more comfortable?" Then we listen again and ask more questions until we're sure that we've truly heard and understood the parent's perspective. Maybe after that meeting we will have come to an understanding. But if we don't come to an agreement in that moment, we keep talking at drop-off and pickup, we e-mail each other, and we may meet to talk a second time. All the while that we are talking and listening and asking honest, open-ended questions, we are building trust and strengthening our relationship. This creates fertile ground for successful conversations in the future.

Here's an example. In our program, we honor and share the story of Dr. Martin Luther King Jr. on or near his birthday. We use our persona dolls to tell stories about his life, and we highlight some of the books in our library that tell his life story. We share the concepts of unfairness and fairness and standing up for something or someone you believe in. We feel strongly that Dr. Martin Luther King Jr.'s life and story are important for children in the preschool years. One year a teacher had taken out one of our favorite books, *Martin's Big Words*, and she began to read. We always edit this book a bit as we read, adjusting it for the particular group of children, because as with most books about Dr. King, *Martin's Big Words* mentions the fact that King died at the hand of James Earl Ray. It often happens that one of the children will share that Dr. King died "because he was shot by a gun." A child said that very thing that day.

The day after the teacher read this book to her group, I received an absolutely furious e-mail from one of our pre-K parents. She was livid that the assassination of someone had been introduced to her child at school. She was just as upset that we were talking about dying at all. She wrote in her e-mail that she could not believe we would talk about this without notifying her first, and she told me that we had lost her trust. We, of course, were devastated. But instead of avoiding a difficult conversation with her, I immediately called the parent and asked if we could meet.

During the meeting, I listened while she reiterated how upset she was that we would introduce the concept of death without her permission. I listened some more and told her how sorry I was. Then I asked more questions and learned that her father, her son's grandfather, had recently died. She shared how devastated she was and how frightened her son now was that he might die or that his parents might die. This was a very, very tender issue for her. We ended our meeting with a plan that (1) I would round up all of our books about Dr. King so she could familiarize herself with them; (2) we would not read this particular book to her son without her permission; and (3) she would spend some time in the classroom while we talked about Dr. King so she could learn more about our activities and the conversations the children participated in. This agreement didn't mean that the parent was entirely happy. She learned that Dr. King's death by a gun had been brought up by a child in her son's class, but learning this did not make her feel better. She did not want us to read most of our books about Dr. King to her child again, and we honored that wish. But by respectfully and compassionately listening to her during our initial meeting and in ongoing conversations, we were able to continue our exploration of Dr. King's life and message in the classroom in a way that this parent felt comfortable with.

When teachers and program leaders commit themselves to respectful, thoughtful exchanges of ideas and work together to create a system that's comfortable for everyone, we create something truly remarkable. This is not a simple task, because holidays are so important for most people. Sometimes it takes many, many conversations and a lot of practice in humbly and sincerely listening to other people's perspectives. Doing so gives us practice in negotiating and give-and-take; these skills honor the diversity in our programs and wider community. What better modeling can we offer our children?

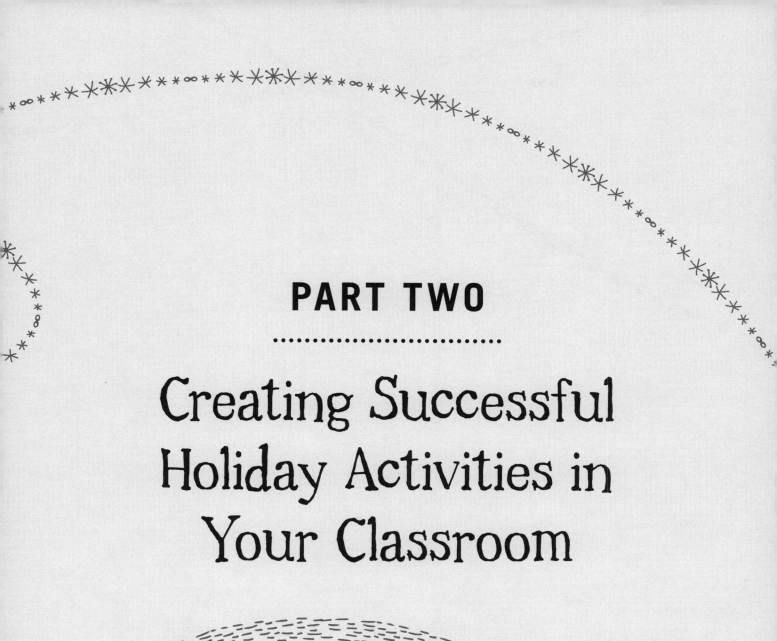

PART TWO

Creating Successful Holiday Activities in Your Classroom

CHAPTER 2

Use Developmentally Appropriate Practice

Acknowledging and validating children's and families' holidays in the classroom can be done in a variety of ways. These range from the very simple validation of what children share about their home lives to more intentional planning and orchestrating of activities. Now it's time to step into the classroom and talk about how to create holiday activities that are relevant and amenable for everyone.

The main ingredient for successful holiday activities is the same as for all good early childhood education programming: understanding developmentally appropriate practice and then planning engaging activities that are meaningful to children and meet their developmental needs. But for some reason, when it comes to holidays, it's all too common to lose sight of everything we know about early childhood curriculum planning. For example, you know that three-year-olds' concepts of time are very limited and generally tied to familiar, actual events, such as when they wake up in the morning or what comes next on the daily schedule. Yet it's common for teachers of three-year-olds to introduce units about the first Thanksgiving, an event that happened hundreds of years ago. Similarly, many early childhood educators work hard all year long to provide art activities that are process oriented. Yet many of these same teachers encourage children to paint red, heart-shaped cutouts at Valentine's Day, to glue cotton balls on bunny shapes at Easter, or to make hand prints on tie shapes for Father's Day presents. These teacher-directed, product-oriented crafts don't nurture children's self-expression, and they surely don't help them develop the higher-level skills of curiosity, creative thinking, problem solving, imagination, and innovation that are so important for twenty-first-century thinkers.

REVIEW CHILDREN'S DEVELOPMENTAL STAGES

When you're planning holiday activities, it's worthwhile to review the abundance of material about the cognitive stages that young children progress through: Janice E. Hale, Lilian Katz, Jawanza Kunjufu, Wade Nobles, Carol Brunson Day, Jean Piaget, Lev Vygotsky, and Amos N. Wilson have made great contributions to our understanding of how young children develop and learn. The 2009 National Association for the Education of Young Children (NAEYC) publication *Developmentally Appropriate Practice in Early Childhood Programs Serving Children from Birth through Age 8* is another important resource.

Children develop at different rates and learn concepts at different times, but most go through the same stages at roughly the same age. Here's a general, year-by-year profile of how children ages two to five understand and respond to holidays. Use this information to guide you in planning age-appropriate activities.

Holiday Ages and Stages

Two-year-olds

★ enjoy being with their families on holidays;

★ can catch excitement from adults but don't understand what holidays are;

★ may be overstimulated or upset by too much change in routine.

Three-year-olds

★ view holiday celebrations in terms of their own family's experiences;

★ are egocentric and think that everyone celebrates the same holidays they do, in the same ways;

★ need to see their families' special holidays reflected in their school environment, especially holidays that aren't highly visible elsewhere;

★ learn from holiday activities that are concrete, accurate, and connected to their own experiences;

★ understand and respond to the feelings that holidays bring rather than to the reasons they are celebrated;

★ may not remember anything about a particular family celebration from last year.

Four-year-olds

★ continue to view holidays primarily in terms of their own families' experiences;

★ continue to need to see their families' special holidays reflected in their school environment;

★ may remember a celebration from last year and look forward to it;

★ begin to realize that some people celebrate holidays other than their own and celebrate in different ways;

- can talk about similarities and differences among holidays that connect to their own experiences;
- understand simple, accurate information about the meanings of holidays.

Five-year-olds

- enjoy celebrating holidays with friends as well as with their own families;
- continue to need to see their families' special holidays reflected in their school environment;
- enjoy preparing for celebrations by making special foods, decorating, and other traditions;
- want celebrations to be consistent ("like last year");
- understand that people celebrate different holidays and enjoy learning about them;
- begin understanding the historical or social reasons why a holiday is celebrated.

WORK WITH CHILDREN

Here are some ideas for sharing holidays with children in different age groups.

Working with twos

It may not be appropriate to talk directly about holidays with children younger than two. For two-year-olds, the focus might be on a decoration they can look at and touch, a food item they can taste and smell, or familiar holiday music they can listen to. If these ideas sound appropriate for your children, invite their families to bring in something from home that their children might recognize and connect with the holiday. It could be a few evergreen branches, cookies (or a recipe for cookies you can make with the children), pomander balls (oranges with cloves in them), a diva (lamp for Diwali), a kinara (candle-holder for Kwanzaa), or some music. Avoid explaining much about the story behind the holiday to children in this age group—limit discussions to a small amount of information. For example, you might say, "Molly brought evergreen branches from the Christmas tree at her house to share with us. I'll put them on the table here so you can touch and smell them," or "This is the kinara that Michael and his family light during Kwanzaa. Maybe we'll light it at naptime and watch the candles glow," or even more simply, "This is music from Maya's house."

With twos and even older children, it's often more helpful to wait until after a holiday to have relevant discussions. At that point, very young children's experiences with their families are still fresh in their minds, and their stories about what they did at home naturally emerge.

Working with threes

Threes are ready for simple activities that reflect what their families do at home. They are still very sensorily oriented and need opportunities to taste, smell, touch, and listen to materials to make them meaningful and developmentally appropriate. Cooking and baking are favorite activities for most threes. Consider inviting a family member to share a recipe or, better yet, to lead the children in a cooking activity! Many children of this age also love to sing. Holiday-related songs that children or families share may be appropriate circle time activities. Discussions about the story behind holidays at this age should be simple and relevant to the ways children celebrate at home. You'll probably find a few children who want to talk a lot about their holiday, while others are less interested and are ready for a new activity. Three-year-olds' attention spans and ability to remember what happened last year are limited. They love books and may be quite interested in holiday-related ones, especially those they bring from home.

Working with fours

Fours are ready for conversations about holidays, especially their own! Many of them can remember family celebrations from last year and are likely to be involved in putting up decorations and making other preparations for this year's holidays at home. They are also ready to begin talking about the different holidays people celebrate. Try making a pictorial graph with them that shows how many children in the room celebrate Christmas, Santa Lucia, Hanukkah, Kwanzaa, Solstice, or new year's days during the winter months. In the spring, you might graph Passover, Easter, Nowruz, and St. Patrick's Day. In the fall, Día de los Muertos, Yom Kippur, Rosh Hashanah, Thanksgiving, and Halloween are just a few of the appropriate days to graph. Books are a wonderful way to represent and introduce holidays at this age. Fours love to be read to and to "read" themselves. Songs are a favorite too. Invite families to share favorites from home or from their own childhoods.

Art activities should be open ended and focus on process over product. Provide materials so children who want to make gifts (anything they choose) can do so, wrap presents in handmade wrapping paper, or create cards or decorations. Fours also enjoy sociodramatic play and are eager to role-play holiday events and happenings when given the opportunity. Consider putting holiday-related props in the house area. Some examples are empty Valentine candy boxes, miniature flags from a variety of countries, gourds, pumpkins, a cornucopia, fancy dress-up clothes, cookie- and cake-mix boxes, candleholders (kinara, menorah, diva, advent wreath), a mini Christmas tree, evergreen branches, dreidels, and pictures of individuals and families celebrating.

Working with fives

Fives like to plan and can handle longer-term projects. If you choose to have an elaborate holiday-related activity, such as a party or other event, fives often enjoy the brainstorming, orchestrating, and problem solving that go with it. Consider posing the idea to them at circle time or at the lunch table, and if the children are interested, make a list of all the things you will need for the party or other event. Talk about what needs to happen and assign working groups where, for example, group 1 is responsible for refreshments, group 2's job is to make invitations, group 3 is responsible for decorations, and so on. With a project like this, opportunities abound for working on small-motor skills (making invitations), math (counting how many places to set), science (baking), large-motor skills (putting up decorations), and social development (working together, problem solving, assigning roles).

Even with this older group, be sure to limit planning and celebrating to only a few days. Ask families to help by coming in and working with one of the groups or by donating or lending materials from home. Fives love to talk about the way they do things at home and enjoy bringing in special decorations or books to share with the group. Fives also like to talk about the fact that different people celebrate different holidays and the many ways that people celebrate the same holiday. Their interests open many opportunities for expanding their understanding of the concepts of similarity and difference.

KEEP HOLIDAY ACTIVITIES IN CHECK

Too many holidays coming too often and bombarding children with food, decorations, and music is a problem in many programs. While such activities are exciting, they can be overstimulating to young children and lead to neglecting their need for familiar, predictable routines. The following are some basic strategies for corralling holiday activities so they are meaningful and fun but don't take over the curriculum.

Talk about rather than celebrate holidays

Not every holiday activity must mean a party. Often it's more appropriate to hold discussions or read books about a holiday or to have family members talk about how they celebrate at home. Here's an example.

In one child care program, many families celebrate Chinese New Year. In honor of this holiday, Lisa's family brings in a Chinese calendar, Nicholas brings in a book about Chinese New Year, Wesley brings in some Lai See (red envelopes with lucky money inside, traditionally given out on Chinese New Year), and a couple of families bring in miniature paper lions similar to the life-sized ones they'll see at the Lion Dance in Chinatown next weekend.

At circle time, the teacher talks a little about the holiday these families will be celebrating. The class shares the paper lion Mei-Ling's family brought in, and Mei-Ling describes how last year she was afraid of the huge lion head that the dancers carried during the parade, but how she won't be this year. Then the teacher reads the book Nicholas brought about Chinese New Year. The discussion concludes with Wesley distributing the Lai See to the children. No additional activities are planned. Occasionally the children ask to have Nicholas's book read to them again.

This approach works especially well when a holiday requires attention but is not developmentally appropriate to delve into. For example, children who attend programs housed in public schools may notice pictures of past U.S. presidents on bulletin boards and may ask about these men. You may want to answer their questions and offer a simple explanation of what Presidents' Day is about, but because these men lived long ago and don't have particular relevance to the children's daily lives, preschoolers will not understand much about them. It's not useful to explain the holiday in great detail or to plan activities around such a holiday.

Fit holidays into your regular routines

Introduce activities that allow you to adhere to your usual routines as much as possible. Holiday activities that last for more than a day or two, that include a lot of sugary snacks, or that include coaching children to memorize songs for a presentation can be too much for young children. Set up holiday art or decorating activities during your regular free-choice or activity time. Learn songs together as you usually do, and invite families to participate in a sing-along instead of a pressured performance. Throughout holiday activities, observe children closely to make sure they are not becoming overstimulated by too many people, activities, or special foods.

Avoid centering classroom themes around a holiday

It's best not to make any holiday the entire focus of your curriculum for an extended time. In some programs, for example, teachers turn December into a gigantic holiday activity. This approach not only overstimulates children, it also leaves out a lot of other wonderful activities and curricular themes that are meaningful to and reflective of the children. Children who don't celebrate that particular holiday feel left out for a very long time.

Steer away from activities that scare children

Young children are often frightened by masks and by people dressed up in costumes for Halloween. This is partly because of their difficulty in distinguishing between reality and fantasy. They may be afraid of the lion's head carried by dancers in the Lion Dance performed at Chinese New Year or of a live Santa Claus. Look for ways to avoid the scary aspects of these rituals and still create opportunities for fun. For example, instead of inviting children to come to your program wearing their own costumes and masks, provide a wide variety of dress-up clothing and materials for making masks at school. Introduce a small model of the lion carried in Chinese New Year dances instead of a large version.

Offer activities that calm children and that focus on process

Holiday-related projects that allow for individual process and creativity provide a nice balance to more hectic activities and large social gatherings. Here are a few examples of activities you can offer:

★ Supply materials so children can sponge-paint or spatter-paint on newsprint or construction paper to make homemade wrapping paper for holiday gift giving.

★ Create a card-making center for any holiday. Include materials like card stock, scrap paper, doilies, metallic paper, markers, stickers, glitter, glue, scissors, staplers, old holiday cards, used wrapping paper, ribbon, rubber stamps and pads. Children can make cards to give away or just experiment with the materials.

★ Invite children to work with clay to create candleholders. Provide clay, sequins, buttons, and glitter. Use clay that dries quickly so children can paint their holders a day or two later. This fits well with holidays that share the common theme of light, as many December holidays do.

★ Water play, digging in sand, and making and molding playdough are calming activities that are appropriate for holidays. To make such activities more festive, try adding holiday-related colors to sand or water in the sensory table or spices to playdough. These sensory experiences may trigger holiday thoughts or memories for some children.

Offer a variety of open-ended materials

For art or craft projects, combine holiday and non-holiday possibilities that allow children to create anything they choose. For example, if you are setting out tissue paper and pipe cleaners so children can make paper flowers for Cinco de Mayo, include additional types of paper, fabric scraps, and glue for collages. Or supply plastic bottles and liquid starch along with the tissue paper so children can make "stained glass" vases.

Provide a selection of holiday-related and other activities

To meet children's developmental needs, make sure activities are available every day that address all areas of development, including language, math, science, small- and large-motor, creative, cognitive, and socioemotional development. But instead of trying to fit all of these into a holiday theme, consider making only one or two of the activities holiday related. The remaining ones can focus on other topics that are relevant and interesting to children, such as changing seasons, new babies, spaceships, or growing things.

CHOOSE APPROPRIATE CONTENT

As an early childhood educator, you know how to use the best of an activity or material and leave the rest. When you read books, you leave out inappropriate passages, and you alter songs so that the little white duck is sometimes a girl and sometimes a boy. Instead of throwing away puzzles that show Asian children with slits for eyes, you use a permanent marker to make the eyes a bit more almond-shaped.

The same should be done with holiday activities. You can pick and choose aspects of a holiday to focus on without losing its essence or meaning. This can be especially useful when ensuring that activities are developmentally appropriate.

Sometimes a new angle on a holiday is all that's needed to make it more suitable for your children. Here are ideas for creative approaches to a few holidays that may otherwise present problems.

Mother's and Father's Day

Mother's Day and Father's Day are very special for some families. Children naturally enjoy making things for members of their families, and gift making for Mother's or Father's Day is a natural extension of this. However, given the diversity of families in our programs, traditional ways of celebrating these days may no longer work. Encouraging children to make gifts for mothers on Mother's Day can be very hurtful to children whose only parent is their father or grandmother. Similarly, putting out materials for children to make Father's Day gifts doesn't work for children who have two moms and no dad. You can avoid putting children and families into uncomfortable positions by celebrating "Family Day" instead. This makes it possible for every child to be included. Make materials available so children who want to can make gifts or cards for anyone in their family: mother, father, grandparent, uncle, brother, godmother, stepparent, foster parent, big sister or brother, and so on.

Valentine's Day

Valentine's Day has become very influenced by commercial interests. This is unfortunate, because this holiday celebrates friendship and caring, values that are meaningful to young children. One program in Southern California has modified Valentine's Day and calls it Appreciation Day instead, emphasizing meaningful themes while avoiding commercial influences (ReGena Booze 1988). Before they celebrate Appreciation Day, the children make a list of everyone in the school community who helps to make their days easier. The list includes people like the secretary, the director, the cleaning crew, the handyperson, the gardeners, the person who cooks the meals, and others. Teachers talk to the children about how lucky they are to have these special people helping to take care of them and making sure that everything that needs doing gets done. A day or so before Appreciation Day (which takes place on or around February 14), the children make and deliver invitations, inviting all of these people to come to their classroom for muffins, juice, and other treats. A group of children and adults bake muffins for the party and put them out on the table just in time for the guests to arrive.

Thanksgiving

Thanksgiving is a difficult holiday to present to very young children for several reasons. First, it recognizes an event that happened hundreds of years ago, too long ago for young children to grasp. Second, it relays a one-sided version of history. Third, it usually reinforces misinformation and negative stereotypes about American Indians. One way to make this holiday meaningful for young children and to avoid its inappropriate aspects is to focus on the universal themes of harvest and thankfulness. These are two themes that children know about and can relate to.

You can introduce activities about food and where it comes from. Discussions can follow about children's favorite foods and all the things they are most thankful for. Use these discussions as opportunities for science, math, and language arts activities. Here are some examples for extending the themes of harvest and thankfulness:

★ Take a field trip to a nearby grocery store, farm, or vegetable stand. Buy vegetables to take back to the classroom, and make soup from them.

★ Cut open a pumpkin, squash, and gourd, and separate the seeds from the flesh. Invite children to sort and count the seeds. Make a graph to see which vegetables contain the most seeds. Try baking the seeds and having a taste test. Set aside seeds to be planted in spring in the classroom's garden.

★ Make homemade pumpkin or sweet potato pie.

★ Wash and bake potatoes or make mashed potatoes.

- ★ Make popcorn.

- ★ Invite children from another classroom to come over one day at lunchtime for a Harvest Party.

- ★ At circle time, hang up a big piece of paper that says "Things We Are Thankful For," and invite children to add to the list (ReGena Booze 1988).

- ★ Make book-making materials available so children can write stories about foods and other things they are thankful for.

The overriding theme here is that people in all cultures and countries celebrate and are thankful for food. They are also thankful for having family, friends, and a safe place to sleep.

Martin Luther King Jr.'s birthday

This is an important federal holiday because it celebrates a man who struggled alongside others to make laws fair for all people. It also opens the door to discussing other people in the civil rights movement. For this holiday to be meaningful to young children, you must explain and observe it in ways appropriate to their level of development.

Prepare for this day ahead of time. Commemorate Martin Luther King Jr., other activists past and present, and the concept of social justice throughout the year so children don't associate them solely with this holiday. Before the holiday arrives, talk about what *fair* and *unfair* mean. Ask the children for their ideas about unfairness. You will probably get answers like "When someone teases you," "When someone won't hold your hand on the field trip," "When everyone gets three crackers and you only get two," or "When someone tells you you can't play." Then tell the children that sometimes rules and laws are not fair, either. Explain that a long time ago, some laws said that people with brown skin couldn't do the same things as people with white skin. People with brown skin had to drink from separate water fountains, eat at separate restaurants, and go to separate schools. In response to this unfairness, many people worked very hard to change those laws. Martin Luther King Jr. was one of them.

When the holiday arrives, show a picture of Martin Luther King Jr. as an adult, or read a book like *Martin's Big Words: The Life of Dr. Martin Luther King, Jr.* Remind children of their discussions about fair and unfair, and tell them that Martin Luther King was one of the people who didn't think those laws were fair, so he and a lot of other people who agreed with him tried to get the laws changed.

Some children may raise the question of if or how Dr. King died. This may be a sensitive point for some families, and I recommend that you discuss this issue with parents and guardians before the holiday. Let them know that the question of how Dr. King died is a common one. Share with families the words you usually use with children to describe how he died. One possibility is to explain in simple language that some people were very mad because they didn't want the laws to be changed, and one person shot Dr. King with a gun, and he died. Find out if families are comfortable with this approach or if they have other ideas. Consider families' input and wishes before you decide on the words you'll use.

Good-bye parties and birthdays

Marking important events in children's own lives, such as birthdays and graduations, with new rituals can make them even more meaningful. Many programs have developed their own ways to honor these events. For example, graduation ceremonies bring closure to a year or more of experiences at school or child care and help children prepare for their next step.

Asking very young children to put on a performance or to sit still while waiting to receive diplomas may be developmentally challenging for them. Instead, some programs celebrate transitional events with good-bye potlucks to which each child brings a favorite food for sharing with the other children and families in the group. In one preschool program, the move from the three-year-old to the four-year-old classroom is celebrated with a crossing-over ceremony. Teachers place a ribbon across the entrance to the new room, and the children symbolically cross over the ribbon to their new class (ReGena Booze, interview with author, April 1992).

Instead of, or in addition to, cupcakes and singing on birthdays, some programs provide a ritual at circle time in which the birthday child passes around a pot of soil. Each child pushes a seed deep into the soil and makes a wish for the birthday child's upcoming year. The sprouting seeds symbolize wishes that may come to fruition. Another ritual involves reading a special book at circle time that the birthday child's family donates or shares in honor of their child's special day.

Remembering developmentally appropriate practice helps you change your holiday activities for the better. In the next chapter, I'll discuss ways to help you reflect individual children's and families' experiences in your holiday practices.

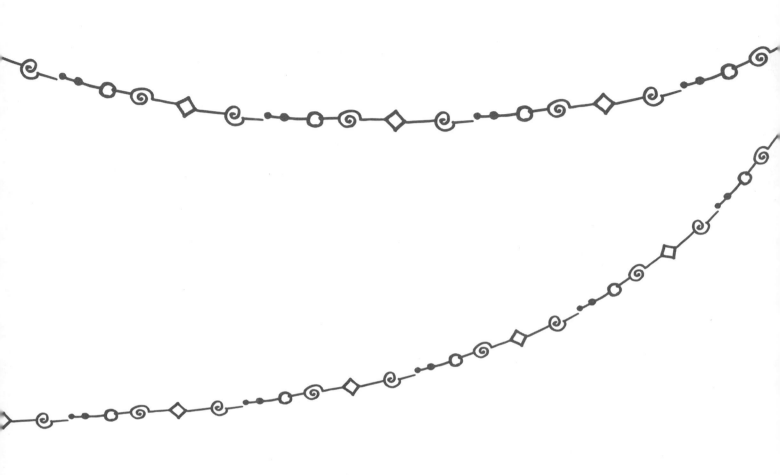

....

CHAPTER 3

Reflect All Children's Experiences

One of the most important considerations when designing your holiday curriculum is ensuring that your activities are culturally and individually appropriate for the children in your program. Such activities reflect children's home experiences and center on materials, information, and practices that are already familiar to children.

CHOOSE ACTIVITIES THAT REFLECT HOME

Many educators are aware that culture is part of a child's identity. Everything we do is affected by culture, including how we talk; how we dress; how we eat our food; where, when, and how we go to sleep; and how we are disciplined. Our culture also informs what holidays we recognize. What is celebrated by children and their families, how we celebrate, when, and with whom are all influenced by culture. In essence, culture is a part of everything all human beings do. Even though it may be hard to see or difficult to define, it is there. When children are in situations that are culturally familiar and consistent with their own experiences, they feel more comfortable and secure. In these situations, they can expect and predict that certain things will happen in particular ways.

All components of the early childhood program should be culturally relevant for children and families. When children walk through the classroom door every day, they should find elements of the room that look, smell, and feel familiar to them. This standard holds true for all components of the curriculum, including holidays. That means activities and discussions must reflect what is celebrated at home and how it is done. When this is accomplished, holiday activities are connecting, empowering, and validating for children. The most valuable activities are those that mirror children's home lives and accurately portray the way their own families celebrate. Involving children's families as much as possible in planning and implementing activities is key to making this work. Participation from parents and guardians makes holiday activities more authentic and meaningful for everyone.

Having most or all of the holiday activities emerge from children and families is a good practice. Instead of planning activities yourself, talk to families who celebrate a particular holiday and invite them to be the source for ideas, materials, and activities. This approach ensures that holiday activities are culturally and individually relevant and reflect families' beliefs, perspectives, and customs.

Here are effective ways to involve family members in your activities:

★ Encourage families to share information about their holidays and how they celebrate (see Gather Information from Families in chapter 10 for ideas on communicating with families).

★ Ask families for ideas about activities appropriate for their and other children.

★ Welcome family members who are willing to lead an activity, such as cooking a holiday dish with the children or helping to decorate the classroom.

★ Ask families for materials that you can use for classroom activities, such as recipes, music, or printed text for special holiday songs.

★ Invite families to loan items to the program for sharing during circle time: decorations, children's books, holiday cards, candleholders, and other holiday-related items from families can enrich your classroom celebrations.

★ Communicate to families ahead of time about what you are planning to do in the classroom so they can contribute or voice their concerns.

Culture throughout Your Program

Your curriculum activities and practices should reflect children's daily lives. The following are just a few of the many methods you can use to ensure that all of your families are reflected in your program every day:

★ Post pictures of children and their families on your walls.

★ Put books on the bookshelf whose main characters are of the same culture as your children.

★ Keep baby dolls in the dramatic play area whose appearances are similar to those of the children in your classroom.

★ At circle time, talk about the different kinds of family structures that are present in your program. Read books and hang pictures that represent those family units.

- ★ Provide foods for snacks and meals on a daily basis that are similar to what children and families eat at home.
- ★ Include cooking utensils, empty food containers, and articles of clothing in the dramatic play area that come from or reflect those in children's homes.
- ★ Talk to children in their home language.
- ★ When feeding children, putting them to sleep, disciplining, or showing affection, be sure to interact with them in ways that are consistent with how their parents or guardians care for them at home.

WORK SENSITIVELY WITH FAMILIES

Be respectful and sensitive when you invite families to participate in your program. Make sure you don't unintentionally offend or alienate them by making assumptions or acting inconsiderately. (Read Evaluate Your Home/School Relationships in chapter 7 to review establishing good communication with families.) Consult books about holidays, talk to people you know who celebrate those holidays, or make use of other resources to gather information before you talk to a family. Ask if what you have learned accurately reflects the ways they practice their holiday and what aspects of it they would be interested in sharing with your group. Remember not to assume that every family who celebrates a holiday does so in the same way.

Holidays can be stressful, especially those that are celebrated during December, when the pressure is on to buy, buy, buy and to create the extravagant celebrations depicted in mainstream media. These times can strain families' financial resources and place many demands on their limited time. Be sensitive when you ask families to participate. Avoid asking them to pay for anything if you think money may be an issue. Respect that they are probably busy too. A strategy you can use with families under financial or time stresses is to ask them for ideas about items that would be appropriate for classroom activities, then borrow or purchase these items and bring them in yourself.

 Caution

Be aware that holidays can be sad and depressing times for some children and families. Divorce, death of a loved one, illness, or the annual reminder of an earlier loss can add great stress to an otherwise festive time of year. Do your best to support families who are struggling with these issues. Don't make assumptions. Remember that you may or may not know about some of these situations.

CREATE BALANCE

Society sends strong messages about which cultural and religious holidays are considered most important. Government agencies, banks, schools, and most businesses are closed for Christmas but not for Passover. They are closed for Thanksgiving but not for Kwanzaa. As a teacher, you send similar messages to children and families with the amount of emphasis, time, and interest you give to each holiday in your program. Make it an important goal to put equal emphasis on the holidays of every religion and culture represented in your classroom. Doing so demonstrates to children that all of their holidays are equally important and valid.

In practice, presenting holidays in an equal, balanced way is difficult. There are two main reasons. First, all of us possess more information about (and maybe more interest in) our own holidays. Second, we may have to work to find information, materials, and other resources for holidays that are not part of the dominant culture. Decorations, music, videos, children's books, adult books, wrapping paper, cards, and other items for holidays like Easter, Thanksgiving, Halloween, and Christmas are easy to find. Locating resources for holidays such as Têt, Diwali, or Ramadan is more challenging. When the majority of families in your program celebrate a popular holiday and only a small minority celebrates another, the odds of receiving more input, ideas, and resources for the majority's holiday are much greater. You'll need to dig harder to treat everyone's holidays equally.

Nonetheless, it's your job to create a balance that helps all children feel equally validated. Here are some strategies to help you do that.

Do your homework

Fill in the gaps, bring in materials, plan activities, and/or share information about the holidays that are celebrated by only a few children in the program or that are scarcely represented in your community. Use whatever resources you can find to portray these holidays accurately and equally. Talk with families, read books, visit communities where these celebrations take place, visit local community resource centers, and go to libraries.

Work to counter inequalities

You can also help by directly addressing the imbalance in holidays that children see around them. This fosters the development of their critical thinking skills. For example, in December, if the children in your program celebrate the dominant-culture holiday of Christmas, you can say, "Sometimes at this time of year people think that everyone celebrates Christmas. But there are many holidays that people celebrate. Not everyone celebrates Christmas" (Kay Taus, interview with author, April 1992). You can continue by explaining to them, "At this time of year, most TV shows are about Christmas and most store decorations are for Christmas, but there are other holidays at this time of the year that seem to get left out, and that makes some people sad."

Don't ignore majority holidays

On the other hand, the answer to balancing holidays in the classroom is not to ignore the most popular holidays, such as Christmas, just because they already receive such widespread attention. Christmas is an important and wonderful holiday for many people, and children who celebrate it deserve validation in their early childhood program.

AVOID BALANCE TRAPS

Avoid these three common pitfalls when you're trying to create a fair balance among different holidays.

Surface-level changes

Don't allow yourself to believe you're being inclusive when your practices are no different than they've always been. This often happens with December holidays. Many teachers proudly proclaim that they include Hanukkah, Christmas, Solstice, and Kwanzaa in their programs, and they may try hard to do just that. But a closer look shows that Christmas continues to be the most emphasized holiday. This is what is happening, for example, when a large classroom bulletin board reads "Happy Holidays," and its decorations include red and green stockings, a cutout paper Santa Claus, decorated paper Christmas trees, and a few snowflakes. Another example is a program that holds its first annual "Holiday Party" instead of its former "Christmas Party." But the only decorations are a live Christmas tree and a few cutout dreidels, painted blue and hung on the walls. For entertainment, one of the parents dresses up like Santa and the children sing four songs: "Jingle Bells," "Rudolph," "Silent Night," and "The Dreidel Song."

Do you see the problem? What messages are being sent about the relative importance of Christmas and Hanukkah? And what about the other December holidays that aren't even acknowledged?

To avoid this trap, examine what you're doing, and ask others to help you critique your own practices. Then work to equal out any imbalances you can identify, and do a better job of presenting holidays equally.

December-only emphasis

A second balance-related trap in early childhood programs comes from the great emphasis commonly placed on December holidays. It's true that quite a few holidays fall during this month, and of course Christmas is valued by many people. However, many major holidays that are significant to people of other religious or cultural groups occur at other times of the year. Rosh Hashanah and Passover, for example, are two of the most important holidays for many Jewish families, yet these are often ignored or only briefly touched on. Instead, many programs place their emphasis on Hanukkah, a minor Jewish holiday that usually falls in December.

One solution to this problem is to learn how important a holiday is to the people who celebrate it, relative to their other holidays. Then take care to put as much emphasis and excitement into their important holidays, whenever those occur, as you do into those that fall in December.

Exotic versus regular holidays

Even when holidays are given equal time, sometimes one is treated as exotic and another as part of regular life (Derman-Sparks and ABC Task Force 1989). Here's an example of the differences in how exotic and regular holiday activities are celebrated. In the classroom where Rosa teaches, many of the children celebrate the American New Year. Don and Cheryl's parents bring in plastic cups, paper plates with "Happy New Year" printed on them, balloons, and noisemakers. At circle time, all of the children talk about their wishes for the next year, such as "to be five," "to get a new puppy," "for my daddy to find a job," "to move to a house with a pool," "to get bigger," and "to sleep over at Marissa's house." Afterward, some of the children play pretend "Happy New Year Party" in the dramatic play area.

The next week, because Chinese New Year is approaching, Rosa decides to invite dancers to come in and perform a Lion Dance for the children outside on the playground. Although she doesn't know very much about Chinese New Year and doesn't have any resources for talking about it with the children, she wants to expose her children to another kind of new year celebration.

If you have ever seen a Lion Dance, you know that it is very colorful, fast paced, and exciting. The children enjoy the dance and the dancers, who are dressed in traditional costumes, although some of the children are afraid of the large, colorful lion's head with its big tongue. But what are the children learning about Chinese New Year, and how does that compare to the American New Year they experienced and discussed a week earlier? In light of how each of these celebrations was presented, they have probably learned that American New Year is regular—an extension of everyday home and classroom life. The Chinese New Year activities, though fun and interesting, instead convey a message of excitement and difference—a performance by exotic people of their exotic Lion Dance. What can this activity teach the children in Rosa's class about the Chinese children in their neighborhood—who they are, and what they do at home?

Making some holidays exotic is most likely to occur when you're trying to include holidays you know little about or holidays that no one in the group celebrates. (See Include Unfamiliar Holidays in chapter 11 for some ideas about celebrating holidays that you, the children, and their families are unfamiliar with.)

Presenting holidays equally is one of the highest hurdles you face when trying to implement an inclusive, representative approach to your children's holidays. You'll need perseverance and commitment to maintain balance. Your rewards will be time well spent and a more equitable, just, and balanced holiday curriculum.

CHAPTER 4

Consider Religion

It is important to give special care and attention to the religious aspects of holidays. Most holidays, including many national holidays, have strong religious components to them. One of your most challenging and important jobs will be to handle religion in ways that respect families' beliefs without going against the constitutional guarantee of the separation of church and state and without trivializing holidays by losing the essence of their meaning or focusing on their commercial representations.

You will have many issues to consider when making decisions about religion. Here are some steps to help you find answers for your program.

CONSIDER YOUR OWN PERSPECTIVE

You are on a holiday journey that requires constant introspection and self-reflection. Religion is a part of culture and has a strong impact on the way people see the world and on their daily lives. (This is true even if you choose not to practice a religion.) It is important to be able to separate your own religious beliefs and any biases that you might have about other beliefs from your work with children. Your primary job is to meet the needs of all the children in your care, those whose religion is similar to yours and those whose religion is different. Remember that supporting and respecting children's and families' beliefs doesn't necessarily mean you agree with them, but such support is essential in helping all children develop to their fullest potential.

To be able to provide this support, you must understand your own strong feelings and beliefs about religion. Ask yourself the questions in the box What Are Your Thoughts about Religion? on the next page. Challenge yourself to honestly explore what your feelings are regarding religion in the classroom. Meet with colleagues or your director or supervisor to discuss your thoughts.

What Are Your Thoughts about Religion?

Ask yourself the following questions to get in touch with your own feelings and beliefs:

★ Do you consider yourself a religious or spiritual person?

★ How important is your religion or spirituality to you?

★ What place do you feel religion has in the classroom?

★ How comfortable do you feel talking about the beliefs of other religions?

★ Do you think teaching religious values is the teacher's job? The family's job? Both?

Don't be surprised if you react personally to matters of religion. It is a foundation for some people. It's easy to become sensitive or defensive if a practice you believe in is challenged or omitted from the curriculum. That is a common reaction, but be sure to think before deciding if and how to respond. Another common response for teachers who are struggling to become more sensitive regarding religious issues is to go to an extreme in the other direction, becoming highly critical of the beliefs and practices of their own religion. While it is good to be aware, it won't necessarily help you or the children you work with to negate your own strongly held beliefs.

MONITOR YOUR OWN RESPONSES

Once you've done the initial checking-in with your feelings, your ongoing task is to examine your comments and reactions to issues as they come up. Do you show respect for other people's beliefs? Can children sense that you are uncomfortable if they talk about God? Think about some potential responses you can give to children so that you are not taken by surprise when they ask questions about religion. Practice your answers with a coworker or your supervisor. Strive to be accepting and inclusive in all your comments.

IDENTIFY YOUR PROGRAM TYPE

Take a close look at the nature of your program. The kind of program you teach in will set the parameters for the decisions you can make about religion.

Public schools

All early childhood programs that receive public funding and/or are affiliated with any public organizations must comply with the First Amendment of the U.S. Constitution, which guarantees the separation of church and state. The principle of separation was created to ensure that the government cannot dictate what religion is right for everyone. It guarantees religious freedom and the right of people to choose. So if you work in a public school program, or in one that is funded by the federal or state government, such as Head Start or a state university laboratory school, you are legally restricted in the degree to which you can incorporate religion in your classroom. (If you are not sure how your program is funded, now is the time to find out.) If teachers in a public program invite children to pray while lighting Hanukkah candles, they blur the roles of church and state and may be violating the First Amendment.

However, there is wide variation in the way that administrators and teachers define the separation of church and state. For example, in some programs, teachers cannot mention holiday names such as Christmas or Hanukkah and must use the word *holiday* or *winter* to refer to anything related to December celebrations. There are winter parties, holiday music, holiday cards, and a winter break. In other programs, it is acceptable to talk about Santa Claus and Christmas trees but not Jesus.

Some teachers feel it is okay to talk about religion if children bring up the topic first. Others say it is never allowable to talk about religious stories or teachings. These educators believe teachers should always defer to children's parents or guardians when children ask questions about religion. There is a constant debate over how far teachers can go. If you teach in a publicly funded program, be sure you know what your program's regulations are and what guidelines the administration has set forth before going further.

Religion-based schools

If your program is affiliated with a church, temple, mosque, or other religious entity, then you have a whole different set of considerations. If your program has clear goals and rules about what religions and what aspects of religion should be included, your job is a little bit easier. In most Jewish programs, for example, it is usually expected that all of the major Jewish holidays will be observed. This is not something teachers must seek approval for from families or coworkers. Instead, it is generally spelled out in the program's mission statement and in the written policies and procedures that families receive when they enroll their children and that staff receive when they are hired.

What is a little bit harder to decide in religion-based programs is whether or not to include holidays that are not specific to the religion to which the program adheres. In some programs, holidays from other religions and cultural groups might not be celebrated per se, but they might be mentioned and a little bit of information about them might be shared with children. In other programs, the holidays of other religions are not mentioned at all.

Private, nonsectarian schools

If yours is a private program with no relationship to a public agency or a religious entity and does not receive public moneys, then you have more freedom legally to include the religious aspects of holidays. This may actually make decisions about religion more difficult for you. When the separation of church and state doesn't apply and the focus of the program isn't on a particular religion, your range of ways to honor religious holidays multiplies.

CONSULT YOUR PROGRAM'S PHILOSOPHY

Whatever your program type, your individual program may already have a written philosophy about religion. A written philosophy provides guidelines for answering children's questions about God(s) and religious and spiritual issues. It also shapes your approaches to curriculum and what kinds of material purchases you can make (such as children's books), and it makes clear which practices are acceptable and which should be avoided. Check your written policies and procedures, especially the staff or parent/guardian handbooks for your program. It certainly makes your work easier if a policy is already in place. If your program doesn't have a policy about religion, perhaps it is time to gather with staff and administrators to write one.

REFLECT ON YOUR GOALS

The type of program you work in also influences your goals for children regarding religious holidays. Are they

- ★ to teach the values of a specific religion?
- ★ to validate children's familiar cultural experiences?
- ★ to help children understand the vast diversity of what and how people celebrate?
- ★ to help children understand the importance of religion in some people's lives?
- ★ to teach children a bit about the religions of all children and families in the program?

Your answers to these questions will influence your practices.

WORK WITH FAMILIES

The key to any successful integration of religious holidays into your classroom is to work closely with families as you decide if, when, and how to talk to children about the religious aspects of holidays. This information will be an important guide as you plan activities and discussions. If your program already has a policy in place on how religion is generally handled, make sure you review it before you speak with families. (Review Evaluate Your Home/ School Relationships in chapter 7 and Select Your Methods in chapter 10 for ideas on communicating with families.) The Sample Family Questionnaire about Holidays in appendix B, page 169, shows one way to give information and solicit feedback. You should also talk with families individually or bring up the topic during home visits.

When you discuss religion with families, you may discover that some of them object to your including religion in holiday activities or discussions at all. Others may be concerned that one religion may be presented as the "right" one. Still others may be very excited about the idea of their child being exposed to the religious stories and beliefs that underpin holiday celebrations. Listen carefully to every family's concerns and preferences. Balance their input with your own philosophies as an educator and the parameters set by your program. Discuss the options with your coteachers and director or supervisor and with families to make the best decisions for your program. Keep families abreast of any plans you have to discuss the religious story in a holiday. Make sure to give examples of how you plan to talk about it. In my program, for example, most holidays are discussed in relation to the children and families who celebrate them, so any mention of the religious story or beliefs in the holiday are shared as reflections of those families' beliefs and experiences. Invite parents to talk with you if they have questions or concerns, as you hope they would concerning any area of curriculum.

DON'T TREAT RELIGIONS AS HOMOGENEOUS

Don't fall into the trap of treating the beliefs and practices of any religion as if they're homogeneous. They aren't. The world's most popular religions (Christianity, Islam, Judaism, and Hinduism) span a wide range of beliefs and practices, and those who practice them may view those of believers from other sects or denominations as wrong. Some Christian sects do not celebrate birthdays or Christmas, while others do; some Jewish and Muslim sects do not permit the mingling of men and women who are unrelated by marriage or blood, while others do; some religious sects or denominations forbid certain foods to their members, while others do not. Be sure that whatever religious components you introduce into classroom discussions or activities arise directly from the families in your program so you avoid mischaracterizing religious beliefs and practices you are not deeply familiar with.

WHEN FAMILIES DISAGREE

If some families differ on what they want to see happen in the curriculum, encourage dialogue with them at a parent/guardian meeting that you or your director or supervisor facilitates. It is my strong belief that in most instances a solution can be reached that all parties can live with. However, everyone may have to give a little for the benefit of the whole group. By explaining to families all of the considerations that you are trying to balance and seeking families' ideas, disagreements, worries, and suggestions for how to move forward, you can design an approach that is acceptable to all.

CHOOSE YOUR APPROACH

So, what are strategies for handling holidays that include religion? They fall into two broad categories: avoiding religion or including it, with many variations within each.

Avoiding religion

Steering away from the topic of religion may be a good option for you if your program is publicly funded or if, for other reasons, you and your colleagues prefer to minimize religious discussion in your classroom. But in practice, avoiding religion can be difficult because it is such an elemental part of many holidays. Avoidance can also cause some problems. If you treat a religious holiday as a purely cultural or historic event, you run the risk of diminishing and trivializing the core meaning for those who celebrate it. For example, to most Christians, Christmas is not only about Santa Claus and evergreens, and Jesus is not simply a man who lived two thousand years ago and taught specific doctrines. For them, Christmas celebrates the birth of Christ, who was and is God in human form, a powerful, life-sustaining deity. To some, presenting Christmas is meaningless without acknowledging this aspect.

Still, avoiding religion may be the best approach for your program, and many teachers have successfully presented meaningful holiday activities without a religious component. Here are some strategies they use.

Stressing cultural aspects

When telling children what a holiday is about, downplay the religious story and symbols and stress only the cultural parts of the holiday. When the topic of religion comes up, acknowledge that many families celebrate the religious story in this holiday, then gently refer children to their own families for information. For example, if a child wants to know more about God, tell her, "Let's talk to your dad about this when he picks you up today." At pickup time, help the child explain her question to her father.

Emphasizing underlying values

Talk about the values of love, care, connection, joy of life, sense of wonder, awe, trust, thankfulness, and/or hope that are a part of many religions and their holidays, without directly talking about religious stories. For example, many American Indian celebrations honor the Great Spirit. Spirituality is an elemental component of these celebrations and observances. However, it is possible to highlight values such as family, connections, and thankfulness, which are important parts of the beliefs and activities tied to celebrations, without going into discussion about the Great Spirit. For example, a Cherokee stomp dance is like a prayer to those who participate, and it is a spiritual celebration. However, when a child in the group is talking about the singing and dancing that he took part in at a summer stomp dance, you can support him as he describes the feelings of sharing and togetherness he experienced and avoid focusing on the spiritual aspects.

Highlighting underlying themes

A useful strategy is to focus on the themes or seasonal aspects of holidays, thereby avoiding discussions about religion. For example, some teachers have had success by focusing on the theme of Festival of Lights during the winter holidays and avoiding extensive individual activities about Las Posadas, Christmas, Kwanzaa, Hanukkah, Diwali, or Solstice. Within this approach, having a winter festival gathering can meet the needs of families and staff members who want to celebrate together during the winter months but want to avoid religious discussion in their child care program. (If you choose this option, make sure your party isn't just a Christmas program under a different name. See Avoid Balance Traps on page 47 for my thoughts on this.)

Discussing instead of celebrating

Discussion is good general strategy for holiday activities that also works well for religion. For example, you might have a child in your program who celebrates Las Posadas, a Mexican holiday that begins on December 16. She could share with the children at circle time how her family and other families in her neighborhood celebrate the holiday by reenacting Joseph and Mary's search for an inn where Mary can give birth to Jesus. But don't follow up with activities such as having children act out this procession in the classroom.

When you invite family members to come in and talk about their holiday, ask them not to focus on the religious belief system behind it. For example, someone from a Muslim family may talk to children about Ramadan and explain how during this holiday adults (and sometimes children) don't eat or drink anything until the sun goes down. The fact that Ramadan commemorates Allah's first revelations to Muhammad can be left out.

Redirecting children's discussions

Often children raise the topic of religion. They might want to talk about their experiences going to church at Easter. Because it is important to honor and validate children's experiences outside the classroom, that is okay. However, if someone wants to talk about God or what the priest said about God, you might say, "Yes, some families believe that. People believe lots of different things about God. At home, you and your family can talk a lot about God and what you believe." Then redirect the discussion by asking the child to share something else about this special family day.

Including religion

An alternative approach to minimizing religion is to deal directly with the religious aspects of holidays. Of course, this is only an option in religious or private, nonsectarian programs. It can be tricky to find a way to include the religious aspects of holidays that doesn't concern, offend, or ostracize anyone. But many teachers believe it is valuable and have found ways to do it! They argue that children need this information about holidays and that to avoid giving it risks diminishing the significance and the meaning behind holidays. Others feel strongly that religion is a part of children's cultures and identities, a critical part for some children. If part of our job as teachers is to validate children, they ask, how can we avoid religion?

Figuring out a sensitive approach to including religion is an ongoing process, but it can be done. Here are ideas that other teachers have used successfully.

Telling the religious story

Plan ahead of time how you will tell the religious story of the holiday at circle time or during an activity. Having a plan will ensure that you have thought carefully about how to share the information in sensitive and age-appropriate ways. Your goal is to let the children know a little about the ways that some people who are a part of the class celebrate a particular day and that other people acknowledge the same holiday in different ways. Here are some examples:

★ When talking about Diwali, the Hindu festival of lights, you might explain to children, "On this holiday some people who are Hindu put candles outside their door to help Rama, one of their gods, find his way home."

★ A way to talk about Christmas is to tell children, "This is the day that some people celebrate as Jesus's birthday." To explain who Jesus is, you might say, "Jesus was a baby who grew up to be a leader. He is very important to people who are Christians."

★ When talking about an American Indian powwow, explain that prayers are sometimes said at the beginning and end of the powwows.

Focusing on the family's beliefs

Center your discussions on the ways the families in your program teach and practice the religious aspects of their holidays. Ask families to come in and talk about their beliefs in simple, developmentally appropriate ways. Invite parents or guardians to bring in an object or perform part of a ritual that children can observe.

Letting discussions emerge from the children

Another straightforward approach is to let questions about religion emerge from the children, then answer them directly and matter-of-factly. You will still have to plan ahead so you are prepared to answer questions accurately, but this approach ensures that children only get the information they are asking for.

Points to Remember

As you know, the issue of religion in an early childhood program is very sensitive. To make sure you are doing the best job you can, remember these essential points.

1. Keeping discussions and activities about religious holidays developmentally appropriate can be especially challenging, because the stories, values, and messages of different religions can be particularly abstract and difficult for young children to understand. Make sure that your discussions and activities about religion do not frighten, confuse, or frustrate children; make sure they are meaningful and understandable. Use simple, straightforward language. (See Telling the Religious Story in this chapter for examples of how to talk to children about the religious aspects of holidays.) Whenever possible, bring in or borrow objects that relate to the holiday to give children something concrete to see and hold.

2. Tread very carefully when talking about religions or religious beliefs. Defer to children and their families for information about their religions and what they believe. This is especially important for religious beliefs different from your own; however, even among people who practice the same faith, you still may find some differences.

3. It is extremely important to use the words *some people* when talking to children about the beliefs and practices of a particular religion (ReGena Booze, interview with author, April 1992). For example, "Some people believe that . . ." or "On this holiday, some people . . . ." Be careful not to put forth any religious belief or practice as the one that everyone in the class believes and participates in. (In some religious programs, it may be appropriate to do this, but in those where some children are of other religions, you must be sensitive to these differences.)

4. A fine line exists between talking about a holiday that has a strong religious component and teaching the religion. For example, Christmas carols like "Joy to the World," which refers to Jesus as the Lord and the earth's king, are religious and, some would say, teach the values of the Christian religion. Be sure to avoid activities that might teach religion, unless that is your intended goal. If a child or family member wants to re-create a ritual that they practice at home in your classroom, help the other children understand that they are guests at the ritual. Observing and discussing rituals are more appropriate for children than participating in them if the rituals aren't ones that their own families practice or believe in.

CONSIDER ISSUES OF ACCURACY AND BALANCE

Many teachers hope to celebrate diversity by bringing unfamiliar holidays into their classrooms. When these holidays have a strong religious component, it's particularly important to think them through first because of the possibility of treating them inaccurately or offensively. If you do choose to include an unfamiliar religious holiday, use the strategies in chapter 10 to help you implement them appropriately.

This is especially important for American Indian religious rituals. Activities such as sand painting, creating a drum circle, burning sage, and using and wearing feathers are all sacred, spiritual rituals in American Indian groups. There is a certain protocol for these rituals and how they occur with regard to the roles of men and women, who can participate, and what the rituals mean. To re-create them in the classroom with the intent of participating in an "American Indian activity" is inappropriate and offensive unless the activity is led by an American Indian child or that child's family. This would be similar to holding Christian communion in the classroom.

Another common problem arises around the issue of balance. It's important to treat religion and religious holidays in consistent ways. For example, if you tell the religious story of one holiday, be sure you are able to tell the religious stories of other holidays with equal accuracy and depth. If you are not able to do this, you convey to children that the story you know is the one that is important. In fact, some educators believe you should not tell children which religion (if any) you adhere to, because as their teacher, you have so much influence on their developing values and attitudes (Bill Sparks, interview with author, April 1992). If you aren't familiar with the religious story behind a particular holiday, find someone who can give you the necessary information before you talk about it with the children.

Also be aware of your degrees of comfort or discomfort with different religious holidays, and make sure you approach them consistently in the classroom. For example, if you are introducing discussions and activities around the religious aspects of Passover, which celebrates the time long ago when Moses led the Jews out of slavery, don't limit your Easter activities to eggs and bunnies because you are uncomfortable talking about Jesus.

Refer constantly and consistently to your goals for holidays as you venture forward in planning and implementing holiday activities. Don't worry about making mistakes. They are inevitable. Just be willing to be self-reflective and constantly evaluate your practices (see chapter 12, "Assess Your Holiday Activities," for information about evaluating activities).

CHAPTER 5

Address Stereotypes and Commercialism

Young children are strongly influenced by the advertising and other media messages that surround them. They may believe that stereotypical images offer accurate and true information about other people or even about themselves. They may feel that their own holidays or families are not as good as others if their home celebrations don't live up to the images they see on television.

As part of your commitment to help children develop to their fullest potential, you have a responsibility to help them recognize and reject these unfair images and messages. By actively talking about and, in some cases, taking action against stereotypes and mass commercialism, you can encourage the development of critical thinking and empowerment in the children and families you work with. You can protect the self-esteem and self-image of children who are threatened by these messages, and you can help them learn accurate information about people who differ in some ways from themselves, as well as develop skills for interacting with others.

 Caution

Acknowledging that a holiday includes stereotypes does not mean you need to avoid it altogether. Holidays have positive, worthwhile aspects, some or all of which may be important to the children and families in your classroom. By addressing the stereotypes in these holidays, you make it possible for the underlying, positive values or messages of holidays to shine through.

UNDERSTAND STEREOTYPES

A stereotype is a widely held but fixed and oversimplified image or idea of a particular type of a person or thing. Stereotypes are hurtful because they demean and dehumanize individuals and groups, perpetuate prejudices, and teach misinformation. They are not only damaging to the people stereotyped but also to all the children who grow up with false information about history and who absorb inaccurate and hurtful "facts" about the lives of others. Let's look at some common stereotypes in our national holidays.

Columbus Day

Columbus Day retells only the European side of the historic event it commemorates and ignores the American Indian perspective. It misinforms by saying that Europeans "discovered" America, when thousands of people and vibrant cultures already existed here. These native peoples were often enslaved or killed by the invaders, their land stolen, and entire tribes killed by the diseases the Europeans brought with them.

Halloween

Halloween brings with it some hurtful images and messages. The color black is popularly associated with bad and evil through emphasis on black cats, black bats, and black witches' costumes. Senior women are portrayed as green-faced, wart-nosed, evil beings. Such depictions leave lasting impressions on children and shape their ideas about people. For example, it is very common for young children to be afraid of elderly women. When asked why, they often say, "Because she looks like a witch." Similarly, the negative connotations of the color black, which persists year-round in images and phrases such as *black-clothed villains*, *black sheep*, *devil's food cake*, and *blacklist*, to name just a few, affect children's feelings about things and people that are dark-hued, most significantly people who are African American (Black).

Thanksgiving

Like Columbus Day, Thanksgiving is popularly depicted from the perspective of European settlers and leaves out that of American Indians. What is commonly portrayed as a time of friendship, neighborliness, and thankfulness was in fact the beginning of lost land, broken promises, diseases, and death for many Native peoples.

Popular versions of Thanksgiving also include abundant stereotypical images of American Indians, who are portrayed inaccurately and hurtfully as half-naked, uncivilized, and grunting people. Commercial greeting cards and decorations frequently depict animals dressed up as Indians and Pilgrims, images that are dehumanizing and disrespectful.

> **⚠ Caution**
>
> It is hurtful and disrespectful to allow children who aren't American Indian to wear "Indian" costumes for a holiday celebration or at any time. Cultural identity is something people are born with and a large part of who they are. Dressing up as American Indians is offensive, just as it would be to dress up as African Americans or Italian Americans. In the proper context, it can be appropriate for children to dress up to play the role of a particular individual (such as Martin Luther King Jr. or Rosa Parks during the Montgomery bus boycott). Of course, it is appropriate for children to use costumes to play out occupations, such as mommies or train engineers, but it is not acceptable for them to dress as "at-large" members of a cultural group.

Researching stereotypes is a good way to help you understand more about them and why some people find certain holidays offensive. Use the resources in appendix A such as Michael Dorris's "Why I'm Not Thankful for Thanksgiving," Patricia G. Ramsey's "Beyond 'Ten Little Indians' and Turkeys," and Louise Derman-Sparks and Julie Olsen Edwards's book *Anti-Bias Education for Young Children and Ourselves.*

These and other resources can also help you identify your own biases. Challenge yourself to identify the stereotypical messages you have absorbed. What did you learn from holidays in school and the media when you were a child? Spend some time talking with your coworkers, a support group of concerned teachers or parents and guardians, anti-bias educators, or your supervisor about holiday stereotypes before you talk with children about them. Work on raising your own awareness first.

ADDRESS HOLIDAY STEREOTYPES

Addressing stereotypes in effective, age-appropriate ways takes attention and planning. Examine your holiday ideas and activities for potential stereotypes and bias. Evaluate your plans, then think about how you will proceed. Here are strategies to help you.

Consider the developmental levels of your children

Before you can begin to counter stereotypes with your children, be sure they are ready. You'll have the most success getting your message across when children are at least three or four years old. At this point, they are actively absorbing negative images and messages from holidays and other media, and they are ready to talk about them.

One way to find out if children are developmentally ready to talk about holiday stereotypes is to interview them. Their responses will help you know what to do next. For example, sit down with them at circle time and ask, "What are you learning about Indians?" (You may have to use this term instead of *American Indians* at first.) If the children don't reply or respond in unconnected ways that don't really answer the question, they may not be ready. However, if you get responses such as, "They kill people, they don't wear shoes or underwear, they dance around a fire and go '*Woo, woo, woo,*'" then you know they are picking up negative messages and it's time to undo some of what's been done. Quite a few good books are available today that accurately depict contemporary American Indians. Reading these books and talking about the pictures of American Indian people in their daily lives can help to dispel some myths and address stereotypes.

Help children acquire accurate information

Children need accurate information about what people really look like, how they really feel, and what events really happened in history to help them counter stereotypes. Provide them with developmentally appropriate information. Give them time to process it, and answer their questions simply and honestly. For example, explain to children that stories about and pictures of mean, ugly witches make some senior women feel sad. Sometimes children who read these books and see these pictures think that all women who are old enough to be grandmothers are mean witches. It hurts older women's feelings when children are afraid to talk with them, hug them, or hold their hands because they think the women are bad witches.

Encourage children to think critically about stereotypical images

During holidays, point out to children that "there are pictures (or messages or stories) about this holiday that are not fair" (Louise Derman-Sparks, interview with author, May 1992). Over time, children can learn to look at images and ask themselves if they see anything in them that is unfair or hurtful to people. This question can expand their already growing sense of fair and unfair and help build their cultural sensitivity.

Adding something to the children's environment or bringing in a book is one way to start a conversation about images that are unfair. For example, many teachers have built up a collection of stereotypical Thanksgiving cards and wall decorations. Bring these in and compare and contrast them with photos of real American Indians living today. Talk with the children about how the cards and wall decorations might make people who are American Indian feel. You might also use a persona doll that is American Indian to talk about feeling sad at Thanksgiving and to explain that the doll's family doesn't celebrate this holiday and why.

Make cultural respect, sensitivity, and fairness a yearlong theme

Avoid the trap of talking about groups only around a holiday that stereotypes them (for example, older women in October or American Indians in November). Discussing some groups of people only in terms of their holidays is one form of the tourist approach. Instead, help children learn about people from various cultural groups all year long. Focus on people's day-to-day lives and the ways that these are similar to and different from the everyday lives of your children. This way, talking about a group and how they are misrepresented or stereotyped in a holiday is only one of the meaningful conversations you have about them during the year.

TALK WITH FAMILIES

Include discussions about stereotypes in your ongoing communication with families about holidays, well before those holidays arrive. Share any information (written, verbal, or both) about hurtful messages and images. Explain to them how you plan to address such issues with the children, and ask for their ideas and feedback.

Consider holding a meeting with parents and guardians to talk further about your concerns and your planned approach. Get the support of your director or a mentor or consultant with expertise in this area to help you explain the issues involved. Remember that some families may feel sad, angry, or defensive if the holiday you are talking about is one that they celebrate. Emphasize that you will not negate the holiday but will celebrate its positive aspects with the children. To help them understand the importance of addressing these issues, be sure to point out that absorbing negative messages about cultural groups hurts all children—those who belong to the groups being stereotyped and those who don't. Negative messages can affect children's growing self-esteem and self-identity and impair their developing ability to understand and interact with people who are different from them.

ADDRESS COMMERCIALISM

The emphasis on buying things at holidays frustrates many people. It minimizes the underlying story or message of holidays and focuses instead on what to purchase to make you and your family happier. It can also put unnecessary pressure on families with limited financial resources and can make children whose holiday celebrations feature fewer things feel inferior.

Some holidays seem to have been overtaken by commercialism; Valentine's Day, Halloween, Thanksgiving, Christmas, Easter, and St. Patrick's Day are clear examples. Hanukkah is beginning to be affected as well. Reflect on your goals for holidays and your overall classroom goals for children. If these include validating children's experiences, making holiday activities enjoyable, or promoting connectedness among children and families, you'll need to counter commercialism and materialism. Here are some strategies to try.

Talk with children about the underlying messages of individual holidays

Focus children's attention on the meanings behind holidays. Tell them a little bit about the historical story of the holiday if they are older than three or four. For example, explain that Thanksgiving is a day for being thankful for the things we have and the people we care about, or that some people celebrate Christmas to remember when a very special baby named Jesus was born many, many years ago.

Explain the symbolism behind the decorations children see at holidays

Shiny red hearts, shamrocks, Easter eggs and bunnies, jack-o'-lanterns, turkeys, and Christmas trees permeate children's environments during holiday seasons. Simple, concrete information about the meaning of these symbols can help children put the holiday and its purpose into perspective.

Remind children that holidays are times for thinking about others

Provide opportunities for children to create homemade gifts for people they love or people in need. This is appropriate anytime. Remember to avoid teacher-directed crafts and instead provide open-ended materials that allow children's creative juices to flow.

Help children think critically about television commercials and other advertising

Explain to children that ads are made to encourage them to buy certain food and toys so companies can make money. (For more information about the media and the advertising industry's effects on children, see Nancy Carlsson-Paige and Diane E. Levin's *Who's Calling the Shots? How to Respond Effectively to Children's Fascination with War Play and War Toys.*)

Help children develop realistic expectations about gifts

Talk with families about what their children's expectations should be, and ask how they would like you to reinforce these. This may be particularly important if the families in your program can't afford or don't choose to provide the kind of holidays portrayed in the media, including some books. One way to handle this is to remind children about their own families' practices. You might say, for example, "At your house, you get one big present and one little present.

That's the way it is at your house. At other people's houses, it's different. Some people get no presents because they don't celebrate Hanukkah or Christmas or any other holiday at this time of year. And some people get a lot of presents. You celebrate Christmas, and on Christmas morning, you get one big present and one little present."

Counter the commercial message that having more means being valued more

Media reinforce the story that Santa only brings presents to good girls and boys. Sadly, this damaging story can lead children to think they are bad if they receive few or no presents. Here's a possible response if you run into this situation: "I believe that all children are good. I don't think that being bad or good is what causes you to get presents or not. I think that children get presents in lots of different ways because people celebrate different holidays in different ways. Some children celebrate Christmas and get a lot of presents on Christmas morning. Some children celebrate Christmas and get a few presents on Christmas Eve. Some children don't get any presents. Some children don't celebrate Christmas at all. But none of that means children are good or bad." At the same time, be careful not to undermine any family's wish that their child continue to believe in magical or mystical beings like Santa Claus or St. Nick.

RESPOND TO FAMILIES' CIRCUMSTANCES

A common, difficult situation is discovering that a family who celebrates a holiday such as Christmas doesn't have the money to buy any presents. If appropriate, talk to the family about this. Ask what words they use to explain the situation to their child. If they need ideas, brainstorm possible ways that they or you can talk about this with their child. Work with your colleagues or your supervisor to come up with strategies for responding to questions from other children who do get presents about why this child does not. Also ask your director or supervisor if your program has developed strategies for helping families in financial need by referring them to agencies and programs that donate goods and gifts or by participating in a gift donation program at the school or center. Treat this issue with respect and sensitivity.

HELP CHILDREN STAND UP TO BIAS

With the support of families and teachers, children can learn to take action against unfair images or messages they're exposed to during holidays. As you uncover the stereotypes in holidays with children, be sure to give them some tools for doing something about these. Here are some tools that encourage children to take action against hurtfulness.

Write letters

Invite children to send letters to card companies or stores telling them how they feel about hurtful cards, decorations, pins, or buttons for holidays such as Thanksgiving or Halloween. Children can also suggest alternative ideas for these products. Have the children dictate what they want you to write, then they can all sign their names to the letter.

Modify popular stories

Help children suggest new words for books about Columbus's "discovery" of the Americas that tell a more accurate story, and include the perspectives of the people who were already living here. Insert new sentences or paragraphs into existing books about Columbus, or write your own classroom book with the children.

Help children talk to families

Support children in explaining to their families what they've learned about how "Indian" Halloween costumes hurt the feelings of people who are American Indian and how witch costumes teach unfair things about senior women. Send home an article for families that further describes the problems. You might use sections of Patricia G. Ramsey's *Teaching and Learning in a Diverse World*, Stacey York's *Roots and Wings*, or other adult materials provided in appendix A.

Whatever activities you use, it's important to support and acknowledge children each time they point out something that is unfair in holiday images. Help empower them by asking if they would like to do something about the unfairness.

CHAPTER 6

Meet the Needs of Families Who Don't Want Their Children to Participate

Sometimes you may have children and families in your program who don't celebrate holidays for religious or other reasons. Families who are Jehovah's Witnesses, for example, typically don't celebrate birthdays or holidays. In other cases, families may celebrate national secular holidays but may not want their child to take part in holidays associated with religions other than their own. For example, some Jewish families may accept the majority of holiday activities in the classroom but feel very strongly that they don't want their children to participate in Christmas activities, such as singing carols in a performance. Muslim families may not want their children exposed to any activities related to Easter. Christian families of some denominations may not want their children to participate in Halloween activities. Families who are uncomfortable with political activism may object to their children participating in a neighborhood peace march in observance of Veterans Day.

Such objections can present a challenging situation for you, especially if holidays and holiday activities play a central role in your curriculum. But a commitment to fairness, respect, and inclusion means finding viable approaches that meet the needs of every child and family. Depending on your situation, your approaches can range from modifying your activities somewhat so families are comfortable with them to eliminating one or all holidays from your program. However, if you work in a program where holiday activities are an important part of your curriculum, such as in a religion-based program, you may not have the option to eliminate holidays. In this case, especially if holidays make up a large part of your curriculum, your program may not be a good fit for a family who doesn't celebrate holidays. You or your director should review your holiday practices and policies with the family, ideally prior to enrollment, and help them make that decision.

The steps in this chapter will help you find solutions that meet the needs of families who don't celebrate any holidays, as well as those families who don't want their children to participate in particular holidays.

EXAMINE YOUR OWN FEELINGS

As with other questions about holidays, your personal feelings and beliefs can be a strong influence when it comes to families who don't celebrate. For some of us, holidays were highlights in our childhoods and continue to be an important part of our adult lives. If this is the case for you, you may feel sorry for children whose family beliefs or values prohibit them from celebrating all or some holidays. You may feel that they are missing out because they won't experience presents or Santa Claus at Christmas, or baskets and colored eggs at Easter. You may feel too that children are being deprived if they don't have birthday parties. You may want to share your own excitement about and enjoyment of the holidays with the children you work with. However, the children's needs may be different from yours.

Some teachers see families who don't participate in celebrations as inconvenient because they upset holiday curriculum plans. This is often the case in classrooms where the majority of the children and families do celebrate and want holiday activities to appear in the curriculum. In this situation, it is not uncommon for caregivers to feel anger toward families who don't celebrate and become concerned about how to meet the needs of "all the other children" when "just one child" isn't allowed to take part.

If you find yourself having such thoughts or feelings, get in touch with whatever might be behind them before you start the process of finding solutions. Remember that your job as a caregiver is to help all children develop to their fullest potential. Remember too that your goal in the celebration of similarities and differences is to include all children. Your commitment to and reaffirmation of these goals are important. Try looking at this challenge as another opportunity to make your classroom a fairer place, one where all ways of living are celebrated.

DIALOGUE WITH FAMILIES

Remember that families may not want their children to participate in specific holidays for a variety of reasons. Whenever a holiday is approaching that you suspect some of the families don't celebrate, or if you think or know that some of your families don't celebrate any holidays, take the time to talk to all of the families and learn if they are comfortable with the activities you are planning. Let those who do not want their children to participate in this (or any) holiday activity know that you would like to work closely with them to make sure you meet their children's needs. Consider talking with your director or supervisor to gain some support and get ideas for working with the families who don't want their children to participate. Then approach the families. You can choose from many communication methods. If you generally hold parent/guardian conferences in your classroom, consider setting up a meeting as soon as possible to talk about this issue. If you are more accustomed to sending home a letter and asking for a response, try that. If you do home visits, you might discuss this topic then. Or you may feel most comfortable talking informally, perhaps when families drop off or pick up their children. (If you use this approach and their children are nearby, show consideration by including them in the conversation.) Whatever approach you use, start the dialogue before the holiday is about to begin.

PROVIDE INFORMATION

When you talk with families, describe your program's approach to holidays. Begin by giving examples of the types of classroom holiday activities you have included in the past. Provide as much detailed information as possible so the families have an accurate idea of your approach. For example, explain to them that when you talk with children about holidays, you always make it clear that some families believe in and celebrate these ideas and some don't. Tell them that you base holiday activities on the ways individual children in your classroom celebrate. If you are in a nonsectarian program, assure them that you do not present one religion as the "right" one. Share examples of specific holiday activities as well, such as making cards as an activity choice for Valentine's Day. Describe the materials that are available—various colors of construction paper, doilies, stickers, and crayons—and explain that some children opt to make valentine cards for friends and families, while others do not. If families enter the program in the middle of the year, share with them the holiday plans you have in place for the rest of the year. Explain that many of these activities are negotiable and that you will make changes to meet their family's needs.

ASK QUESTIONS

The next step is to gather specific information from families about what is acceptable to them and what isn't. Don't assume you know, even if you know something about their background or know other families from the same background. Give each family an opportunity to share with you their individual perspective on holidays and what experiences they want their child to have or not have in your classroom. At the same time, it will help you to earn their trust if you have a little knowledge about their background before you speak with them. A good approach may be to talk to other people or read books about the religious or cultural group the family belongs to. Then ask families if this information accurately reflects what their family believes and practices.

Ask the families questions to further clarify their practices and wishes. For example, if some families are Jehovah's Witness, you might ask: "Should all celebrations be avoided, or only ones with a religious basis? Can your child participate in social justice holidays like Martin Luther King Jr.'s birthday? Are invented celebrations acceptable, such as Backwards Day or end-of-the-year celebrations to say good-bye to graduating children? Is it okay for your children to be present in the classroom when holiday activities are going on? If so, can they participate in any way? For example, if another parent or guardian brings in a treat to share for a child's birthday, can your children participate? Can they sing 'Happy Birthday,' or eat the snack?"

When you talk with different families from the same cultural or religious groups, you may discover that there is variation in what celebrations and activities are acceptable. For some Jehovah's Witnesses, it is acceptable for children to make a pine tree out of construction paper but not to decorate it. Or they may be allowed to make a pumpkin as long as it doesn't have any facial features. For other Witness families, a Thanksgiving celebration may not be allowed, but they may welcome their child's participation in a Harvest Party, where the emphasis is on sharing and preparing good foods and learning how we get these foods from nature (Stone 1991). For still other Witness families, any activity related to a holiday may be more than they are comfortable with. This is equally true for members of other Christian denominations and other religious groups when it comes to certain holidays.

Be sure to listen thoughtfully. Keep an open mind toward all of the information the family shares with you. Building trust and gaining the family's respect will be of utmost importance as you work with them and other families throughout the year. Work hard at understanding the perspective of these families and suspending your own strong feelings.

RECHECK YOUR EMOTIONS

If your practice has been to base much of your curriculum on holidays, you may feel now that you will have to significantly change your approach, yet your efforts may still not be enough for families who don't want their children to participate in any holiday activities. It is hard not to get defensive when this situation arises. Learn all you can, and then take some time afterward to work through whatever feelings come up for you, such as anger or frustration, with a coteacher, director, or a colleague in the field but outside of your program. In the long run, you will realize that because of the changes you make, your overall curriculum will become more reflective and inclusive of all children and families in your classroom.

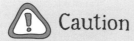 **Caution**

Remember that it is not your job to try to persuade families to raise their children differently. Instead, it is your role to value, respect, and support all families' child-rearing practices. Think about it this way: You wouldn't try to convince a family of vegetarians to begin eating meat (Stone 1991) or try to sway a Christian parent to become Jewish. Your role should be one of support, acceptance, understanding, and cooperation. Use this situation as another opportunity to talk about the different ways families can be.

PROVIDE DIFFERENT OPTIONS

Once you understand families' needs, take responsibility for playing a role in finding solutions. It is not fair to expect families who don't want their children to participate to come up with all of the answers. Instead, brainstorm some possible solutions on your own or with your colleagues. You may find that you need to alter your practices just a bit to make your activities acceptable to all families. The following strategies, also described in earlier chapters, may offer solutions for families who don't celebrate.

Recognize instead of celebrate

Sometimes approaches that teach children about a holiday without asking them to participate in it are acceptable to families who don't celebrate that holiday. This may mean limiting your holiday activities to discussions, reading books, and having family members talk about how they celebrate at home.

Offer many activity choices

For some families, just knowing that their children won't be forced to participate in a holiday activity or be made to feel ostracized for not doing so may be all that's required. In that case, making holiday activities a choice instead of a whole-group or required activity may be the answer. Provide enough interesting options so that children who can't participate in the holiday activity can easily choose another. All they may need is a gentle reminder to choose one of the other activities. It is also helpful to make activities open-ended so that children can use the materials in any way they choose. Then, for example, while some children are decorating paper bag Halloween costumes, a child who doesn't celebrate Halloween can decorate a paper bag mural or a paper bag puppet.

Caution

When providing alternative activities for children who can't participate in a particular holiday, remember that the alternatives that you offer should be as enjoyable as the holiday activities. Remember too that if other choices are offered to one child, they should be made options for every child. That way, no child feels excluded or bad for not engaging in holiday activities that everyone else is doing.

Avoid religion

For some families, avoiding discussion about the religious aspects of holidays and focusing on the cultural aspects may meet their needs. As I mentioned in chapter 4, this is difficult to do because religion is an intrinsic part of so many holidays. Nonetheless, it is possible to de-emphasize religious discussion and avoid religious symbols yet still talk about a particular holiday. Be sure to check with the families in your classroom to find out which parts of holidays they consider to be religious and which you'll need to avoid.

Change your focus

Altering your approach to an activity is another possibility. If, for example, the activity that a family has the most trouble with is birthday parties, request that families save birthday celebrations for home. Then implement another activity in lieu of birthday celebrations. One idea is to have VIP days. On their VIP day, each child gets the spotlight. A variety of pictures of the child and family go up on the bulletin board, along with information about favorite colors, favorite animals, a drawing of where the child lives, and a story written by the child. Similarly, if there are children in the program whose families don't want them to participate in any activities related to Halloween, ask their families to help you come up with a viable alternative. One avenue might be to focus on the themes of harvest or masquerade instead of Halloween.

Consider omitting holidays that are particularly problematic

If you discover that one holiday is particularly problematic for many families in the program, weigh the pros and cons of omitting it from the curriculum. Situations where this approach may be a good option include a program with many Christian families who object strongly to the celebration of Halloween, or a program with many American Indian families who don't want their children to participate in traditional Thanksgiving activities. Consider this approach too, if even just one or two families strongly object to a particular holiday. Since your goal is to meet the needs of each and every child, as well as the needs of the whole group, think carefully about which practice will be best. Consider talking this over with colleagues and your director or supervisor to get ideas and support before making any decisions.

Honor families' requests that their children not be present

A final option is for children to be removed from the room (or stay at home) when holiday activities are going on. This should be a last resort and a solution that the family proposes rather than you. In some cases, however, this may be the only feasible choice if families do not want their children to be present during activities that are holiday related and all other possibilities have been explored. If you must use this approach, make sure the child who is being removed, and the children who aren't, understand that this isn't a punishment for the child who can't participate in the activity. For example, if you go for a walk with a child, invite other classmates to come along so all children realize they can choose whether or not to participate (ReGena Booze, interview with author, April 1992).

COMMUNICATE WITH OTHER FAMILIES

If you think it's appropriate, talk with all families about the adjustments you are making in your holiday curriculum to accommodate families who don't celebrate. In some cases, you might want to include other families in deciding what changes to make. Remind families that as part of your commitment to an individualized program, the curriculum needs to be fair and meet the needs of each and every child. Explain that all families may have to yield some of their wishes in order to enhance your program's culture of fairness and inclusiveness. Keep in mind, however, that your role in this situation can be tricky. It is up to you to ensure that families who don't celebrate (especially when there is only one) aren't made to feel like nuisances because of their values or beliefs. Do not allow other families to make them feel that way. Remind parents or guardians that you regularly modify classroom practices and make decisions based on individual children. Help families see this situation as a valuable learning opportunity for their children and themselves.

SUPPORT CHILDREN

It is important to work with all of the children, those who celebrate and those who don't, to help them appreciate and respect each other's family practices. Children who celebrate national holidays get great validation from stories, television shows, and other aspects of society. Because of young children's egocentric nature, it is easy for them to think that what they do is right. They might even think that other children must be bad, sad, or unloved if their families don't participate in holidays at home. These children need help to understand that there is nothing wrong with children and families who don't celebrate.

Equally or even more important, children who don't celebrate holidays get little or no validation for their practices from our larger society. It is your job to help them feel validated, supported, and welcomed in your classroom.

Working with families, you can also help children who don't celebrate holidays develop strategies for living in a society where holidays play a large role. Encourage families who don't celebrate holidays to help prepare their child for a classroom of children who do. Suggest that families give children words to help them explain why they do not participate in certain activities at school (Stone 1991). Find out what those words are so you can support these children and families. Also ask the parents or guardians to talk to their children about the kinds of activities they will find at school during the holidays. Questions may arise that families can answer better than teachers. Try these strategies for supporting and educating all children around the issue of families who don't celebrate.

Bring in a persona doll

Use a doll at circle time to explain to your group why its family doesn't celebrate a specific holiday or any holidays. The doll can also help explain what it's like to work on different activities or leave the room while others are participating in holiday activities. This is a good technique for giving children who celebrate some simple, concrete information about the beliefs and practices of families who don't. It also helps them to understand what children who don't celebrate holidays might be feeling. For the children who don't celebrate, having a persona doll with a similar identity can relieve some feelings of isolation and some of the pressure to do all of the expl aining about their families' beliefs. This is especially important when there is only one child in the class who doesn't celebrate. (See chapter 11 and Trisha Whitney's book *Kids Like Us* [1999] for more information about using persona dolls.)

Find a book—or write one

If a child in your program belongs to a religion that doesn't celebrate holidays, look for good, sensitive books about other children who belong to this religion. If you are unable to find such a book, make your own. Create a main character who has enough in common with your children so they can identify with her and who follows the same religious practices as the children in your room who don't celebrate. Maybe the child in your book loves to go to school and enjoys soccer, T-ball, and cupcakes; however, birthday parties are hard for her because everyone else gets to eat cupcakes, while she has to wait until the celebration is over to eat hers. Then the character can explain why she can't participate in the birthday parties at school.

Invite family members

You might invite family members who don't celebrate holidays to come in and share with the group something fun that their family does together. This gives other children an opportunity to learn that while some of their classmates and their families don't celebrate holidays, they do enjoy fun things together. They might not celebrate birthdays, but they might exchange presents at other times of the year, take trips to places like the circus and the zoo, and in some families, have a special family dinner together every week. They are not sad, solemn families who never laugh. Having their family members come into the classroom gives children who don't celebrate an important opportunity to be recognized and validated for their families and something they do at home.

PART THREE

....

Plan and Implement Changes

CHAPTER 7

·········

Assess Your Situation

As you begin thinking about changing your approach to holidays, it's important to understand that this is an emotional issue. Holidays are a very meaningful and personal part of many people's lives, possibly even your own. If you feel strongly about holidays for religious or other personal reasons, it may be more emotionally challenging for you to look at holidays in new ways. Similarly, as an educator, you may have devoted a great deal of time, energy, and passion to the holiday curriculum you've been using and are now being asked to change. If this is the case, you may naturally feel defensive or resistant, and this will take effort to overcome.

A second point to recognize when getting ready to change your approach is that you can't do this alone. Teachers, directors or supervisors, and the parents and guardians of the children must all work together to make significant, lasting changes.

This chapter will help you assess yourself and your setting in terms of these issues so you can better understand where you are starting from as you begin to plan for change.

UNDERSTAND YOUR OWN PERSPECTIVE

Self-awareness is important. Whether or not you have strong personal feelings, it's important for you to know what perspective you are coming from when you approach the topic of holidays. Knowing your own values, beliefs, feelings, and possible biases before you get started will make it easier for you to evaluate your current practices and consider new approaches that will better meet the needs of the children and families you are working with. The following questionnaire will help you clarify the thoughts and feelings you bring to this issue. Once you uncover your own perspective, keep it in mind as you sift through the information and suggestions offered in this book.

What Filter Am I Using?

★ Did your family celebrate holidays when you were a child?

★ How important were holidays to your family when you were growing up? How enjoyable were they?

★ Which were your favorites?

★ As a child in school, did you feel the holidays that were important to you and your family were respected? Validated? Considered normal?

★ Did your family celebrate holidays the way you saw them portrayed in the media? Did you feel like you fit into that picture?

★ Did you ever feel excluded either literally or figuratively because of what your family celebrated or didn't celebrate?

★ How important are holidays to you in your adult life? Are there any that are particularly important to you? Any that you really enjoy or really don't like? Or do you avoid holidays all together?

★ What do you really like about holidays? What do you dislike about them?

★ Are any holidays you celebrate as an adult a part of your religious beliefs? If so, which ones? How do they relate to your religion?

★ As an educator, how much of your current curriculum is devoted to holidays? How attached are you to the holidays and activities you have used in the past?

THINK ABOUT YOUR OWN POSITION

There are many players to consider as you go forward. Making successful changes in the way you approach holidays depends on you, your coworkers, your supervisor, your staff, and the children and families in your setting. It's important for everyone to work together. Without an agreement and everyone's support, your attempts to make changes and create consistency will be difficult.

Still, exactly who you involve and their degree of involvement depends on your position and the type of program you work in.

If you are a head or lead teacher, you may have a certain amount of control over your curriculum and how you and your coteachers approach holidays. It is important to gain the support of your director or supervisor and to work closely with coworkers or assistant teachers in your classroom to get their opinions and ideas.

If you are an assistant teacher, speak to your supervising teacher and your director or supervisor, using the approach that works best for you. Let them know you would like to make changes in the way you approach holidays in the classroom. Tell them why. You will need to gain the interest of your supervising teacher, and coworkers if applicable, before going further.

If you are unable to gain the interest or support of your coworkers or supervisor, don't give up. You may not be able to make a sweeping change, but you can still improve the ways you talk to children about holidays and how you implement activities that you do control. Keep a dialogue going with your colleagues at your center or school. Look for support and ideas from outside sources too, such as community colleges that offer anti-bias courses, your local Association for the Education of Young Children (AEYC), or a support group of other educators who want to make changes in holiday practices.

If you are the director or educational supervisor, you probably have the greatest potential for making change in how holidays are approached in your program's classrooms. If you have a lot of control over your educational program, you can initiate change in the holiday curriculum in your setting. Start by sharing information—an article, a book, a conversation with a colleague, or a workshop you attended—about the value in rethinking your holiday program. Ask for input from your staff and families, and encourage them to explore this with you further. Then, once the process is begun, your involvement and your support will remain essential. Teachers need to rely on you for ideas about educating others, gaining information from families, developing strategies for activities, and organizing staff or family meetings.

EVALUATE YOUR HOME/SCHOOL RELATIONSHIPS

Whatever your position, children's families will be an integral part of the process as well. Parents and guardians have critical information that you will need to select and implement inclusive, culturally relevant holiday activities. In addition, they deserve communication about how their children may be affected by changes in holiday curriculum, and you will need their support to successfully put your changes into place. In fact, for many programs the best way to plan for change is to involve interested family members as partners who participate fully in the process of creating a new approach to holidays. (See chapter 9, "Develop Your Holiday Policy.")

If you haven't already established an effective method of communicating with families, asking for information and feedback about holidays may not be the place to start. The topic of holiday inclusion and implementation can be emotionally charged for families, as well as for teachers. Before you can approach this issue, it's necessary to look at your relationships with the families of the children in your care. To help you evaluate, ask yourself these questions:

★ How well do you communicate with families?

★ When do you communicate with them? Do you see them every morning or every afternoon? Do you always talk with them for a few minutes about their child's day?

★ What do you feel comfortable talking about with your families? Can you talk about toilet training, biting in the classroom, tips for handling sleeping or sibling rivalry at home, and so on?

* Do you cross paths with parents and guardians outside of school? Are you comfortable talking with them informally on these occasions?

* Overall, how successful have your interactions with parents and guardians been?

If your ongoing communications with families are not as good as you would like, spend some time working to improve them. Choose a few of the strategies suggested in the next section and try them out for a month or two. Then, once you feel your communication is sound enough, you can begin to ask about holidays.

On the other hand, if you feel that you already have a good working relationship with your families, jump in! It's not necessary to strive for a perfect relationship before asking parents or guardians to become involved in the holiday planning process. But you do need to have a foundation so that asking about holidays won't seem out of place or alarming.

LET YOUR PROGRAM'S STATED VISION AND VALUES PAVE THE WAY

One of the biggest ways I've changed as a child care center director since writing the first edition of *Celebrate!* is that I am now unwavering in my belief that leading from a place of vision and values can transform your program. Once you have developed a set of core values to lead by, you possess the foundation and road map for almost all of the decisions you need to make. For example, because my staff and I value relationships tremendously, I schedule my week knowing that at least 40 percent of each day will be spent in conversation with the many teachers and parents who walk into my office with a need or a concern, or just to talk. I don't regard these moments as lost time but rather as investments in our relationships.

Improving Home/School Communication

Select the strategies that work best for you and your program.

Strive toward daily conversations: Try talking a little with all parents or guardians at drop-off or pickup time. Share a bit about how each child's day was and what activities were available.

Use a communication notebook: If you don't have a chance to see families during the day, try putting a notebook near the sign-in sheet. Parents and guardians can use this spot to leave you notes about their children or to ask questions they need answered. You can respond to their requests by calling them during the day, sending an e-mail, or leaving a note in their mailbox or their child's cubby.

Consider making a family communication bulletin board: Hang a bulletin board in the classroom or just outside. Use it for posting newsletters, the teachers' names and the hours they work, your curriculum, articles about parenting, a wish list of materials for families to donate.

Have a call-in time: Another strategy for keeping in touch with families and communicating the message that you want to know what's on their minds is to set aside a certain period of time (perhaps naptime or your planning time) when they can call you at the center with their questions or concerns.

Hold conferences: If you don't already, begin holding yearly or twice-yearly conferences to talk with families about their children's developmental progress and how their children spend their days in your program.

Spend time in the community: Participate in everyday activities in the neighborhoods where the children and families live. Shop at a local store, visit a park, eat at a restaurant, or go to the post office. Making this effort will go a long way toward building strong, trusting relationships.

LEAD WITH VALUES

Because our program values inclusion and social justice, we weave a fabric of cultural relevancy and anti-bias learning into all of our daily activities, materials, and interactions. These values in turn guide our decision making about enrollment, parent meetings, staff development, holiday practices, and everything else we do.

If you are new to the idea of leading with a vision and developing program values to guide your work with children and families, I recommend that you get to know Margie Carter and Deb Curtis's book on this topic, *The Visionary Director: A Handbook for Dreaming, Organizing, and Improvising in Your Center*, which takes you through the process of identifying core values and putting them into practice. At our center, I refer again and again to one of Margie and Deb's activities for developing core values: during staff or parent meetings, we invite each participant to jot down their ideas in these columns:

WHAT DO **CHILDREN** DESERVE?	WHAT DO **STAFF** DESERVE?	WHAT DO **FAMILIES** DESERVE?

Margie Carter writes, "To maintain a visionary mindset, the operative word here is *deserve*. Focusing on what people deserve keeps you from reducing your vision to merely meeting minimum standards" (2010, 20). Once everyone has jotted down their thoughts, you can go through the process of coming to agreement on perhaps the five most important values in each column. Then set to work crafting values statements based on those values.

The values you create influence everything in your program, including holiday practices. In fact, they make the work of determining how to handle holidays much easier. Recently, for example, I was setting the stage for a review of our holiday policy at a staff meeting. Parents had been invited to join us in our discussion, and our plan was to consider our approach to the winter holidays, which were then just around the corner. I thought we first needed to remind each other why we recognize and include holiday activities that are important to the families in our classrooms.

I started by reviewing our values. Here's what we came up with:

We recognize holidays in this place because

1. We value what is important in children's and families' lives.

2. We value relationships, and we see opportunities for deepening relationships through holidays.

3. We value cultural relevancy and anti-bias practices and the opportunities that holidays offer for furthering our anti-bias goals.

This quick revisit to some of our values reminded us of some of our overarching principles around holiday practices, including these:

1. In general, our approach is one of recognizing, discussing, and sharing rather than actually celebrating holidays.

2. We maintain a connection to seasons and their natural rhythm.

3. We work in partnership with families.

4. We constantly look for opportunities to talk about both similarities and differences in the ways we celebrate (for example, families may celebrate the same holiday in different ways or families may celebrate different holidays altogether).

5. We bring out inherent anti-bias and diversity themes in intentional ways (for example, stereotypes of American Indians at Thanksgiving; working for fairness on Martin Luther King Jr.'s birthday).

6. We use the term *some people* to avoid promoting one holiday, one way of celebrating, or one religion as the correct one.

7. We aim to observe holidays in secular ways, but we do briefly and broadly share the religious stories behind holidays.

8. We intentionally work to ensure that no one is ever excluded. If a family is so uncomfortable with the content of a holiday discussion that they don't want their child to participate in it, we will change what we do rather than exclude a child or family.

The conversation and collaboration with parents that followed this introduction left all of us energized and full of ideas as well as additional questions, which is exactly what should happen. After all, the path to holiday practices each year is a journey that requires regular nips and tucks to meet the needs of everyone in our program. (You can see the final version of our policy in Epiphany Early Learning Preschool Holiday Policy, appendix B.)

If you want to make real changes in the way you handle holidays in your program, I urge you to establish and follow your program's values as a road map to guide your practices.

ACKNOWLEDGE THE CHALLENGES OF COLLABORATION

Working together with colleagues and families is a necessary and valuable process in the effort to change your approach to holidays, but it is also a difficult one. As you begin to make decisions cooperatively, proceed with patience and thoughtfulness. Realize that this is indeed a process and that sometimes you may feel like you're taking two steps back for every step forward. But like any process, the most important thing is to keep on working, to keep your eyes on your goal. The following are some tips and reminders to help you stay on course:

★ Strive to separate your personal holiday needs from the needs of the children in your classroom.

★ It is okay to disagree. The important thing is to open up dialogue and listen to each other with respect and understanding.

★ Keep checking in with yourself about your own feelings, values, and perspectives. This will help you keep your own opinions in view while remaining open to other ideas as well.

★ Always remember that discussions about holidays may evoke strong emotional reactions. Expect to discuss the same issues several times so everyone has a chance to reflect, sort out their thoughts, and come to a consensus. Be patient.

★ Finally, enjoy the process! Take advantage of the opportunities that arise to engage with coworkers and families in meaningful dialogue and the sharing of ideas.

CHAPTER 8

Determine Your Program's Goals for Holidays

Before you can really think about what to celebrate or how to implement holidays in programs for young children, it's necessary to think about why you want to recognize holidays. Like all well-planned curriculum, holiday activities need to have specific goals. Questions such as "What do I hope to accomplish?" and "What do I want children to get out of holiday discussions and activities?" will help you make conscious decisions about the use of holidays.

To develop your list, you'll need to work with colleagues and involve parents and guardians. Read through the steps below first, then work together with others to arrive at agreed-upon goals. Keep in mind that collaboration can be challenging. You might want to review the questionnaire What Filter Am I Using? and the section Acknowledge the Challenges of Collaboration, both in chapter 7, for reminders and suggestions about working together. It might also be helpful to distribute and discuss the questionnaire to get in touch with and understand one another's perspectives.

CONSIDER POSSIBLE GOALS

For me, one of the overarching goals for holidays is to create experiences in which everyone feels reflected and welcome and in which children and adults alike deepen their connections to one another in the classroom. We learn more about, and appreciate and value, the ways that we are both similar to and different from one another. These goals are part of the four anti-bias goals published by Louise Derman-Sparks and Julie Olsen Edwards in *Anti-Bias Education for Young Children and Ourselves* (2010, 4–5).

Anti-bias Curriculum Goals

1. "Each child will demonstrate self-awareness, confidence, family pride, and positive social identities."
2. "Each child will express comfort and joy with human diversity, accurate language for human differences, and deep caring human connections."
3. "Each child will increasingly recognize unfairness, have language to describe unfairness, and understand that unfairness hurts."
4. "Each child will demonstrate empowerment and the skills to act, with others or alone, against prejudice and/or discriminatory actions."

The goals below reflect my program's anti-bias approach. You can decide if any of them fit your program.

To promote connections among children, families, and staff

Holiday celebrations build and strengthen connections between home and school, and among children and/or teachers who share the same holidays. They also can promote a sense of community among children when they learn about one another's holidays and participate in activities together. The connection happens when children realize that they have something in common. When Asma discovers that Hakeem also celebrates Ramadan, their friendship and esprit de corps is strengthened. Similarly, when Linda's mother comes in to make buñuelos for Cinco de Mayo, other children participate and feel included. Through this shared activity, a feeling of community emerges.

To learn about important events in the lives of all children and families in the program

Introducing holidays that are important to children and their families communicates respect and commitment to inclusion in classroom practices. Including these holiday activities in the curriculum provides an avenue for other children and adults to learn about these important events.

To support and validate the experiences of children, their families, and staff

Holiday activities support children's experiences at home and in their communities, strengthening positive feelings about and connections to their families and cultural groups. Plainly, children get the message that what they do at home is valid and worth mentioning at school. This is especially valuable for children and families whose holidays are not usually reflected in media, store decorations, children's books, and other places.

To reinforce connection to cultural roots

Holiday rituals can reaffirm or deepen connections to cultural roots, helping to teach or remind children of who they and their families are. These rituals can also give children a sense of security: they feel comfort in knowing that they will see some familiar sights, taste some familiar foods, and be together with people who are important to them. By including or talking about these same holiday rituals in the classroom, you bring those reminders and feelings of comfort into your classroom.

To celebrate both similarities and differences in children's lives

Holiday activities can show children in direct, meaningful ways that the same holidays can be celebrated differently and that people often celebrate different holidays honoring events and beliefs unique to their own ethnic groups. Activities can also point out to children the similar themes that run through many holidays, such as death, renewal, light and darkness, liberation, and harvest. Most important, holiday activities demonstrate that all holidays are important to the people who celebrate them and must be respected.

To stretch children's awareness and empathy

Learning about holidays that are different from their own is one method for helping children move away from egocentric thinking and become aware of other people's ways of living. It can be especially helpful to children who celebrate the national holidays to learn that what and how they celebrate isn't the one "right" or only way.

To teach children critical thinking about bias

Many holiday images and messages from television, radio, store decorations, books, magazines, and billboards unfortunately perpetuate gender, race, culture, class, and historical biases. Including these holidays in the curriculum offers you opportunities to teach children how to examine what they see and hear for messages that are unfair or hurtful. Activities and discussions can also challenge children to consider the commercialization and mass marketing of certain holidays. These activities can lead children to understand that not being able to afford gifts doesn't make a family bad or less than other families.

To teach activism

Empowering children to stand up for themselves and others is an important early childhood goal. By celebrating social justice holidays like Passover, Martin Luther King Jr.'s birthday, and Mexican Independence Day, children learn about what real people have struggled over in the past to create a better life for themselves and others. These celebrations can lead to discussions about people who are working for justice today.

To give children accurate information about specific holidays

Holiday activities can support what children learn at home and correct misconceptions they may have about other people's holidays. Activities can help children separate commercial depictions from actual history and the lessons behind holidays. Discussions can give children accurate information about the meaning behind the symbols, songs, smells, and holiday artifacts. This has particular relevance for children who are new to the United States and its holidays and do not understand the meaning of the symbols and rituals they see around them.

To mark time for children

Holiday celebrations can underscore certain times of the year by celebrating beginnings, endings, and other significant rhythms, such as seasonal changes. This has particular importance for twelve-month child care programs, in which there is seemingly no beginning and no end to the year.

To have fun

Holiday activities can be enjoyable. They add spice to daily life by providing a break in the usual routine. They can also bring feelings of anticipation, excitement, and magic into the classroom.

CONSULT YOUR PROGRAM'S GOALS

To begin developing your own list of goals for holidays, think first about your program's overall goals for children. You may have broad, overriding goals, such as encouraging self-esteem and nurturing children's development in social, emotional, cognitive, physical, and creative ways. You may also have multicultural or anti-bias goals to help children learn to value themselves and others. And you may have more specific goals, depending on the type of program you are in and what you think is most important for children. In some schools and centers, these goals may be predetermined by administrators, directors or supervisors, or a board of directors, and written into program policies. In other cases, you can determine your own goals.

THINK ABOUT THE CHILDREN AND FAMILIES IN YOUR SETTING

Next, consider the children and families in your program. The goals you choose should be appropriate for their developmental levels, cultural backgrounds, and how similar or diverse they are as a group. For example, if you teach two-year-olds, your goals will be different than if you teach fives. (See chapter 2, "Use Developmentally Appropriate Practice," for detailed information about holidays and development.) If you teach children who are new to the country, your primary goals may be to foster a connection between home and school, validate their home experiences, learn about important events in their lives, and offer information about the United States' holidays they see happening around them.

REFLECT AND REVIEW

Think about and discuss your final list of goals. Keep in mind its importance, because it will steer the rest of the decisions you make about your holiday approach. At the same time, remember that your list can and should change in response to changing circumstances.

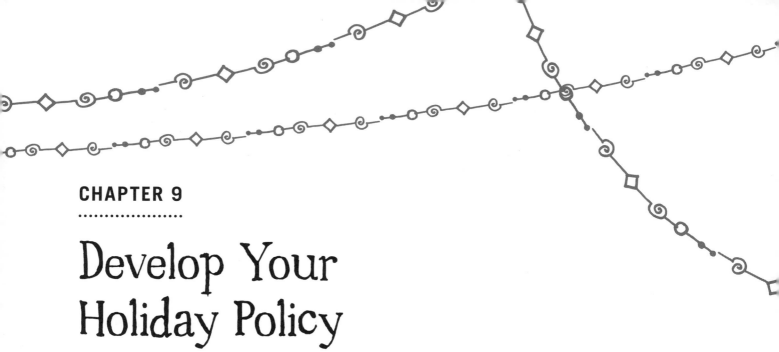

CHAPTER 9

....

Develop Your Holiday Policy

Formulating a holiday policy at the same time that you shape your new approach to holidays can help make your decisions easier in the future. A holiday policy can guide everyone involved in your program to choose, implement, and evaluate holiday activities. The policy must be clear, detailed, and flexible. If you are a classroom teacher, the policy may be applicable to your individual room only. If you are a director or supervisor, your policy may guide your whole program.

Once you put your policy in place, you will always have it to refer to. It can be used to communicate your holiday approach to new staff and families who enter the program, though you should also stress that they can participate in ongoing improvements and transformations of the policy.

Many factors will play a role in determining when and how your policy is developed. You might want to begin developing it while you read through the chapters of this book. Or you might be more comfortable waiting until you've planned and implemented some holiday activities using a new approach so you will have a sense of what works for you.

Building your policy in stages may work best. Try starting by reviewing your past holiday practices. Then develop agreed-upon goals to guide you in changing or improving your approach. Next, talk about how you will make decisions about which holidays to include. Last, give yourself time to work out the nitty-gritty issues of implementation. *Celebrate!* guides you through this process and offers information to help you make decisions.

Whatever approach you choose, remember that developing a holiday policy requires time and effort and will be affected by the successes and failures you experience in your classroom during each passing holiday. Don't be discouraged if it takes three meetings just to make one important decision, or if a whole year passes before you get your policy in writing.

INCLUDE EVERYONE WHO WANTS TO BE INCLUDED

All teachers, assistants, and supervisors who will be affected by the policy and who would like to be involved need to be included in its development. Parents and guardians who are interested in this issue should be included as well. If you don't have everyone's participation, you run the risk of not having their buy-in. When this happens, people may say that they understand and agree with the policy but may then withhold their support and cooperation because they really don't.

It's true that some teachers or directors have developed holiday policies and made decisions about how to handle holidays that work well for them without consulting families and coworkers. This solo approach is sometimes easier than organizing a group effort and working collaboratively with others. If you work in a program where contact with families is limited, or in a part-year program where school starts after Labor Day, you may find it hard to reach decisions collaboratively before the first holidays are upon you. It's also true that educators possess knowledge about child development and working with children in group settings that families may not, so some decisions may be better when made by staff.

Nevertheless, the solo approach misses out on opportunities. One of the most valuable outcomes of bringing educators and families together to talk about goals for holidays is the thoughtful discussions that ensue (Katie Kissinger, interview with author, April 1992). These opportunities to share views and values are essential to programs using an inclusive, anti-bias approach. Holiday brainstorming meetings provide an opportunity for community building among educators and families. People can get to know one another, hear each other's points of views, practice respectful listening, and learn about different values and practices. In addition, families deserve to be involved in curriculum decisions, particularly decisions about how holidays, which are so individual, personal, and important, will be handled. Given the opportunity, families often jump at the chance to have their voices heard and to participate in the decision-making process. The teamwork between educators and families and the shared ownership of the decisions that will emerge will be very valuable.

CHOOSE A METHOD

There are two general models of collaboration for developing your holiday policy.

The facilitator model

In the facilitator model, one person takes the lead and is in charge of organizing the work and producing the final policy. In some programs, this person is the director, a teacher, a parent or guardian, or a community member. The facilitator drafts sections of the policy and circulates them to other staff members and families for comments. Based on that feedback, the facilitator then redrafts and sends out the sections again. The process repeats itself until the facilitator has all of the needed information. The policy is then written. During this process, the facilitator may also call meetings and facilitate discussions, then draft sections of the policy based on that input.

This approach works well because the facilitator, who is ultimately in charge, keeps pushing forward the development of the policy. This model keeps everyone on track, with one person delegating the typing and copying of drafts and supervising the distribution of drafts and the gathering of feedback. It is probably the most realistic and efficient model for many early childhood programs, given their organization and structure. The drawback to this approach is that it can be time consuming for one person and doesn't involve other players as fully as the committee approach.

The committee model

In the committee model, a group of interested teachers, family members, administrators, board members, and other appropriate people meet on a regular basis to develop a policy. In some situations, the committee might put together some recommendations that will then go to another authority, such as the director or board, for final approval.

The benefit to this approach is that it enables many different people in the school community to be involved in the policy in a major way. Programs that use this approach make a strong statement about their desire to include everyone. The drawback to this approach is that it can be unwieldy. Finding days and meeting times that work well for everyone can be difficult, especially if the committee is large. A strong commitment and a lot of collaboration among committee members are necessary so that note taking, typing, copying, distributing, and other tasks are performed in a timely manner. Some committees find it helpful to assign an organizer who takes care of or supervises these tasks, and some may need a point person to help keep them on track and move the process forward.

The primary distinction between the facilitator and the committee approaches is that with the facilitator, much of the information in the policy originates with the facilitator and is then sent out to the school community for feedback. With the committee approach, all information originates within the committee at meetings. You may find that a single approach, an approach that combines the two, or some other model works best for your situation. The most important consideration is to make sure that no one who wants to be involved in the process is left out.

SET YOUR OWN GROUND RULES

Whatever collaborative approach you use to develop your holiday policy, everyone must understand clearly from the beginning which decisions can be influenced by those participating and which will be decided by a person or governing body in charge. It is very frustrating for people to think they are going to have an impact on policy, to put in the effort and time, and only then to find out that someone else really makes all the decisions. Be honest with other educators and family members about what decision-making power they truly have and what they don't. Let them know whether or not everyone will have an equal say. In most situations, there will be a director, teacher, board of directors, parent advisory committee, or someone else in charge who will make some final decisions.

If you are the person in charge, be sure that you know what your bottom lines are before asking for input. If there are certain things you absolutely want in your policy or definitely won't allow, say so at the beginning. For example, if you know that you will not allow violent or stereotypical costumes or decorations at Halloween, say so. If you cannot allow religious activities in your program, make sure everyone knows this before talking about Easter, Rosh Hashanah, or Ramadan.

Keep in mind too that it is likely that not everyone involved in the decision-making process will be able to agree on all aspects of your holiday policy. You or whoever is in charge should think about how to handle this situation if or when it arises.

OUTLINE YOUR POLICY

A holiday policy has many components. Each one answers a question about how holidays will be handled in your individual program. Below is a list of questions to consider as you decide what to include in your policy.

What are the goals and functions of holidays in the program?

What do you want to accomplish with holiday activities in the classroom?

How do these goals relate to the children and families you work with? To your overall program goals and your anti-bias goals?

How important a place will holidays have in the program?

How much curriculum time will they take?

How many holidays will you include each year?

How much time will you spend on each holiday?

How will you make decisions about which holidays to include?

Who will make the decisions?

How will families be involved?

How will information be gathered from families?

What role will teachers play? What role will the administration play?

In what ways will holidays be implemented in the curriculum?

Will you have parties? Decorate? Read books? Play music?

Will you discuss holidays at group meetings, such as circle time?

How will families be involved in holiday activities?

How will teachers get the information they need to accurately portray a holiday?

How will holiday activities reflect the overall classroom goals and specific goals for holidays?

How will you make sure that all activities are developmentally appropriate?

How will you make sure that holiday activities and discussions are connected to children's experiences?

How will stereotypes in holidays be addressed?

How will you handle the religious aspects of holidays?

Will holidays with a strong religious component be included?

Will you talk about the religious component? In what way? Will teachers initiate the conversation? Or must it emerge only from the children?

What is the plan for working with children and families who don't celebrate a holiday or holidays?

How will you make sure that no children are excluded?

What will be the choices for these children?

How will you evaluate the effectiveness of holiday activities?

How will you get input from families about their perception of the success of holidays?

How will teachers and directors or supervisors give input?

What will you do with the information you receive?

On the next page is a sample holiday policy that addresses the components discussed above. Remember that this is only a sample, not a recipe to follow. Because your policy will reflect and meet the needs of the children and families you work with, your policy will probably look quite a bit different.

Willow Child Care Center Holiday Policy

Definition of Holiday Activities

It is important to define holiday activities because the words *holiday* and *celebration* mean different things to different people. For purposes of this holiday policy and to define our holiday practices in the classroom, we define "holiday activities" in the following way.

Holiday activities at Willow can be as simple as reading a book about a holiday and as elaborate and involved as having a party in the classroom with food, decorations, guests, and music. Activities often involve a group discussion about a holiday and how a family celebrates it, or the reading of a book about a holiday. Other times teachers set up open-ended, developmentally appropriate activities for children that relate to a holiday.

Goals and Functions of Holidays

1. To validate children's and families' holiday experiences and traditions at home
2. To expose children to different ways of celebrating the same holiday
3. To expose children to celebrations, traditions, and religions different from their own
4. To foster respect for celebrations, traditions, and religions different from children's own
5. To provide fun and a break in the routine
6. To mark time for children
7. To build a sense of community, family, and togetherness
8. To provide accurate information about holidays in a developmentally appropriate manner
9. To encourage critical thinking about bias and unfairness
10. To provide a stress-free environment

Role of Holidays in the Program

Since we plan curriculum on an emergent basis in a way that reflects children's needs and interests, the exact amount of time we spend on holidays will vary. We use children and families in the program as a barometer to help us decide how much we will do with holidays. We do have some guidelines, however, to make sure that holidays do not take over the entire curriculum. With regard to parties or actual celebrating, we will limit holiday parties to three or four per year. When we are "recognizing" a holiday (that is, having a discussion or reading a book) or providing activities related to a holiday, we might include up to five holidays per month.

For example, on the Friday before Memorial Day, we will talk about the fact that the center is closed on the following Monday and explain why, in two or three sentences. When we are doing calendar every morning, we will talk with children about holidays that just occurred or that are approaching. These recognitions of holidays, however, are no more than a two-minute discussion about what the holiday is called and what it is all about, unless children ask to know more. Similarly, when we provide activities, they will be open ended and one of many choices so they are not the focus of the entire curriculum.

How Decisions Will Be Made about Which Holidays to Include

Individual decisions about which holidays will be included will be made every year and when children and families leave or enter the program.

1. First, teachers and the director will use a variety of methods to determine what holidays are important to the children and families in the program. These methods will include a questionnaire, interviews, home visits, parent/guardian meetings, and daily communication.

2. Then teachers will make a list of any additional holidays they think are important to include. These include holidays they have incorporated in the past, social justice holidays, holidays that are celebrated by the staff, holidays that support overall classroom goals, and holidays whose stereotypes or misinformation provide opportunities for teachers to help children correct wrong impressions.

3. Next, teachers and the director will look at the holidays that children are unfamiliar with. Before deciding to include any of these holidays, teachers will make sure they can introduce them in a relevant, respectful way that connects to children's own experiences.

4. Teachers and the director will then look at the list they have generated so far and decide if anything else should be added or dropped from the list. Together they will make sure that all the chosen holidays meet at least one of the stated goals for holidays and that none of those holidays will offend or hurt any child or family.

How Holidays Will Be Implemented in the Curriculum

Below is a list of general guidelines we follow at Willow as we implement holidays:

1. We are inclusive. We strive to validate everyone and exclude no one. We pay attention to the balance and the importance we put on certain holidays over others. No one holiday is portrayed as more important than any other.

2. We concentrate on reflecting a holiday in a way that is important and relevant to families at home.

3. We work to be culturally relevant in all of our activities. We portray holidays from the point of view of the person or group that celebrates those holidays. If teachers are not of the religious or cultural group that celebrates a certain holiday, we gather information from books and people who celebrate the holiday.

4. We do our own research. Teachers learn what they can about a family's holiday that we are unfamiliar with before asking that family to supply information. This communicates respect and a genuine desire to obtain information.

5. We involve families as much as possible in the implementation of holiday activities and celebrations. We also keep families informed of upcoming holiday activities and events.

6. We are careful to avoid stereotypes when presenting holiday information to children, putting up decorations, and implementing activities. We also are committed to addressing unfairness in holiday images and messages that children may be experiencing outside of the classroom so they learn to recognize bias and hurtfulness.

7. We provide activities that are developmentally appropriate for the ages and stages of the children. Young children need concrete, hands-on activities and simple explanations. We are careful not to abandon all we know about good practices when it comes to holiday activities. We know that teacher-directed art and reproducible crafts that all look alike do not foster creativity or individual expression.

8. We are sympathetic to the fact that holiday time can create hardships for some families because of financial constraints, family problems, and so on. We are careful not to implement any activities that put financial pressure on families.

How Religious Aspects of Holidays Will Be Approached

While teachers won't teach the religious aspect of a holiday or teach one religion or religious holiday as the correct one, we will explain, in a developmentally appropriate way, what the historical meaning of that holiday is if children ask us directly for that information. Religious aspects will be explained matter-of-factly, in simple language. Families will be consulted for the actual language they use when talking about religious holidays to their children. Children will also be referred back to their families for more explanation and in-depth information about religious aspects of holidays. Aside from providing answers to children's direct questions about the religious aspects of holidays, teachers in general will avoid talking about religion without sacrificing the underlying meaning of a holiday. For example, we will explain that Christmas is a time for giving and sharing and Valentine's Day is a day for friendship and caring.

Plan to Work with Children and Families Who Don't Celebrate Some or Any Holidays

We will not celebrate any individual holiday that excludes one or more children. If we have children in the program who do not celebrate any holidays, we will work with all families and staff to come up with a plan for holidays that meet their children's needs so they are not left out.

How We Will Evaluate the Effectiveness of Holiday Activities

We will be constantly reflective of holiday activities we have done in the past and how we might handle holidays in the future. Once a year, teachers, the director, and families will get together to talk about what is working, what isn't working, and to discuss future strategies

PERIODICALLY EVALUATE YOUR POLICY

Like other components of an early childhood program, your holiday policy should be regularly evaluated for its effectiveness. If possible, sit down with colleagues and families every twelve months or so and look at your holiday policy and overall approach to the holidays. Ask each other the following questions:

★ How is the policy working? What are the overall strengths and weaknesses of our policy?

★ Have we been handling holidays in ways that reflect our holiday goals and overall program goals?

★ Is our method working for deciding which holidays to include in the curriculum?

★ How effective are our methods for gathering information from families?

★ Have families been involved in activities as much as we would like them to be and as much as they would like to be?

★ How successful have we been at maintaining a fair and equitable balance among all the holidays? Are children or families getting the message that we consider some holidays more important or valuable than others?

★ How well do we meet the needs of all the children and families in the program, both those who do and those who do not celebrate holidays?

★ Are we satisfied with the way we have been handling the religious holidays?

★ What effective strategies have we developed for dealing with stereotypes in holidays?

★ Are there specific problems we have not been able to solve? What are they?

If families are not able to be a part of your discussion, consider sending out a simple questionnaire like the one on the next page to gather their input. Remember to translate questionnaires into the languages the families speak. Consider asking these questions in an informal interview if some families are more comfortable with that.

Holiday Evaluation Questionnaire for Families

Dear Families,

It's time for us to take a look at how effective our holiday practices have been throughout the past year. Your input is critical to our evaluation process, and we would greatly appreciate it if you would answer the following questions and return the questionnaire to the office by next Monday.

1. Are you satisfied with our overall approach to holidays this past year?
   Please tell us why or why not.

2. What would you like us to add to our practices?

3. What would you like us to stop doing?

4. Did our activities and discussions this year adequately and accurately reflect your child and your family's rituals and celebrations? If so, how? If not, how can we improve?

5. Do you feel that there were enough opportunities for you to become involved in our activities? If not, how can we improve in this area?

6. What suggestions do you have for us in the next year?

Consider holding a family meeting to discuss your findings and to develop a plan for making improvements. Every family may not be interested in attending. That's okay. Welcome those who attend. The important thing is that all families are invited and encouraged to provide feedback in some way.

Be willing to alter your holiday policy to reflect the information you gather in the evaluation process. The holiday policy should be flexible enough to grow as you do and to evolve to meet the changing needs of your families.

CHAPTER 10

Identify Holidays to Include

Once you are clear about your goals for holiday activities, start considering which holidays will help you meet your goals. Of course, how you implement holiday activities will be essential to determining your overall success. First, you need to think about whether specific holidays merit inclusion in your curriculum at all.

You and your colleagues might want to begin this process by evaluating the holidays you have selected in the past. Take out the list of goals you developed in chapter 8, "Determine Your Program's Goals for Holidays." Then, under each goal, write down the holidays you included in your curriculum last year that related to it. Are there any holidays that do not fit any of the goals? You may be including a holiday just because you enjoy it personally and want to celebrate it, not because it is important and meaningful for your children. Are there any holidays that fit only one goal (such as "to have fun"), and don't seem as important to include, given your other goals? Are there any holidays that meet one or more of your goals but that may be hurtful or offensive to any child or family?

After you've reviewed your current practices—or if you didn't celebrate any holidays last year or you just prefer to start fresh—you can begin to work together to develop a list of holidays to include now.

GATHER INFORMATION FROM FAMILIES

If you look back at the end of chapter 8 and your goals list, you're likely to see a strong emphasis on learning about and reflecting children's home experiences. Clearly, to meet these goals, you will need to gather considerable information from children's parents and guardians. Your primary purpose will be to learn all you can about what holidays families celebrate and how they celebrate them so you can be inclusive and reflect families' home practices. Learn more about the religious backgrounds and beliefs of each family, because religion plays such a large role in holidays. Some families may object to their children being exposed to certain holidays, and some families don't celebrate any holidays at all. It's important to learn this. (Chapter 6, "Meet the Needs of Families Who Don't Want Their Children to Participate," offers you ideas and strategies for meeting these families' needs.)

Naturally, you will need to be sensitive and respectful to the families you speak with. Your conversations about holidays must take place in the context of solid relationships between you and families. Turn back to Evaluate Your Home/School Relationships in chapter 7 and decide if you are ready to proceed with the next step in the process.

SELECT YOUR METHODS

When you are ready, begin communicating with families about their holiday practices at home. Many good communication methods are available. Here are examples to choose from or to combine.

Questionnaires

Send out a questionnaire asking families what special days they celebrate at home and how they celebrate them. The more precise you are about the information you wish to have, the better responses you will get. For example, the sample questionnaire on the next page asks for specific information, such as the importance of holidays to families, how families want their holidays to be reflected in the classroom, and other pertinent questions. Be sure to include on your questionnaire an explanation of why this information is needed. Remember to translate questionnaires (and all other communication) into the languages that families use.

Family Questionnaire about Holidays

Dear Families,

Your answers to the following questions will help us greatly in our efforts to develop an inclusive, sensitive approach to holiday celebrations and to plan activities appropriate for your children's ages and developmental levels. Thank you for taking the time to fill this out. Please return it to the office by [*date*].

1. On a scale of 1 to 10, how important are holidays to your family? (The number 1 means unimportant and 10 means extremely important.)

2. What special days do you celebrate in your family? How do you celebrate them?

3. How would you like the program to support or reflect your celebrations? If your family does not celebrate any holidays, how would you prefer us to work with you and your child if/when we have holiday activities in our program?

4. What would you like your child to gain from holiday activities while in our program?

5. What concerns do you have about holiday activities?

6. How do you feel about your child learning about or participating in holiday activities that are not part of your family's tradition? Are there any holidays you would object to?

7. Religion plays an important role in many holidays. While considering these next questions, please keep in mind that our teachers would not teach any religious perspective as the "right" religion; rather we would always say, "Some people believe . . ." or "At Sally's house, they believe . . ."

8. What religious holidays, if any, do you celebrate in your home?

9. How would you feel about your child experiencing in our program the religious aspects of holidays you celebrate in your family?

10. How would you feel about your child being exposed to religious aspects of a holiday that your family may not believe in?

11. How would you like to participate in holiday activities in the classroom?

Family meetings

Hold a meeting to explain to parents and guardians why you want to learn about family holidays. Allow plenty of time, and answer any questions to gain families' trust about how you will use the information they provide. Consider combining this approach with distributing the questionnaires. One strategy to ensure participation is to hand out the questionnaires at the meeting and encourage parents or guardians to fill them out before they leave. You can also individually interview family members who are not comfortable using a written questionnaire.

If a discussion arises about issues like what holidays to include or what parents and guardians would like to see happen in your approach to holidays, be prepared for strong reactions and emotions. You may need to support people who express opinions that are counter to what most of the group feels and wants. Assure everyone that you and/or others who are making decisions will take everyone's feelings and needs into account as much as possible and will strive to meet everyone's individual needs. Offer to meet individually with families to discuss concerns.

Home visits

If you do home visits, consider asking for holiday information then. If you have already conducted all your home visits for this year, keep this strategy in mind when planning for the next year.

Informal conversations

Drop-off and pickup times in schools and child care settings can be good times to gather additional information. E-mailing and phoning parents or guardians at agreed-upon times are other effective tactics. Phone conversations may work very well for some families, especially if they do not have the time to fill out a questionnaire or just feel more comfortable talking rather than writing out their responses.

Community participation

Teachers can learn a lot about what and how families celebrate simply by being present in their communities. If you don't live in the same neighborhoods as your families, make an effort to visit them both during holiday times and at other times of the year. For example, shop in the grocery store, walk down the street, play in the park, and attend a holiday festival or other cultural event that is open to everyone. You will learn a lot about the families' daily lives as well as their holidays if you spend time in their communities. Families will trust and respect you more if they see you regularly in their communities.

SUPPORT RELUCTANT FAMILIES

Families whose holiday celebrations are very different from what they perceive others' celebrations to be may be particularly concerned about how you will use the information you gather. Sometimes these families are reluctant to share information because they are concerned that their children will seem too different if their unique holiday rituals or activities are included in the program. Other families may be willing to share information but will ask that you not plan activities around their special day. Families have myriad reasons to feel this way. Some may prefer that special holiday activities not occur at school so that their child will look forward to the festivities at home. Others may feel it is inappropriate to share certain holiday activities with children who are not members of their own religious or cultural community.

Families must be able to trust that the private information they share with you will be used respectfully and sensitively. Ongoing dialogue with families about the purpose for the information and how it will be used will help to ease their apprehension. But if parents or guardians would simply rather not share information, their decision must be respected and supported.

Points to Remember

As you gather information from families, keep these points in mind:

★ Asking about holidays is only one piece of the overall task of respectfully learning about each family's culture. Finding out about families' day-to-day lives is equally important.

★ If you think families celebrate holidays that are different from yours, learning a little about the holidays before asking for information will go a long way in building trust and showing that your interest is sincere.

★ Don't assume that everyone from an ethnic group celebrates the same holiday or celebrates a shared holiday in the same way. Similarly, be aware that some families who are multiracial may not celebrate all the holidays related to their diverse cultural or ethnic backgrounds. Ask each family to share information so you don't make any inaccurate assumptions.

★ Keep in mind that although at first glance your program may look fairly homogeneous (for example, all European Americans or all Spanish speakers), a deeper look will uncover much diversity. Differences in religion, socioeconomic class, and family styles and practices may be abundant. These differences are important to recognize, learn about, and celebrate.

REVIEW YOUR INFORMATION ABOUT FAMILIES

When you finish gathering information, you can develop your draft list of holidays. Begin by writing down all the holidays that families celebrate at home, those that are important to them, and those that they consent to have you include in your classroom.

You may discover that including all of the special days listed would require having more holiday activities than you want in your curriculum. This is particularly likely if families in your program come from many different cultures or religions. You don't have to include all of every family's holidays, but you should make sure that at least one or two of each family's holidays are recognized. One strategy is to look for a few holidays that are important to many different families and make sure to include those. Remember to recognize the one or two most important days for each family as well.

 Caution

When choosing holidays, some teachers feel that it is more important to include those that are not validated and reflected in the larger society. Since some holidays, especially Christmas, are so pervasive in our society, it may seem unnecessary to include them in the curriculum. But young children don't understand this logic. If Christmas is a holiday that is important to them and their family, they deserve to have it reflected in the program just as much as other holidays. The leaving-out approach might also make some family members feel angry or hurt that your professed sensitive, inclusive approach to holidays excludes them.

Also remember that while it's okay not to include every holiday celebrated by your classroom's families, it is very important to look for a variety of ways besides holidays to represent families' cultures. For ideas, review Culture throughout Your Program in chapter 3.

FIND OUT ABOUT PROGRAM REQUIREMENTS

Some early childhood programs may have policies or regulations in place that will influence which holidays you can celebrate in your classroom. For example, a religious-based program, such as one associated with a church, temple, or mosque, may require certain religious holidays each year. A publicly funded program may restrict religious celebrations but require that some national holidays be recognized. Find out if any rules such as these will affect your decisions, and add these days to your list.

Celebration of some holidays may be expected, though not officially required, by the agency you are in. These expectations may differ, for example, depending on if your program is located in an elementary or high school or on a college campus. In some instances, students or faculty at these schools organize events to celebrate holidays, such as Cinco de Mayo or Halloween. In those cases, it may be important for you to include those holidays in some way.

ADD YOUR OWN CHOICES

Next, add to your list the holidays that you, as an educator, believe offer valuable experiences for young children or that are important for the community in which you work. Here are a few categories to consider.

Holidays that support classroom goals

Selected holidays can highlight the overall goals that you and your children work toward all year and that are relevant for every child in your program. For example, introducing activities for Mahatma Gandhi's birthday (October 2) or International Day of Peace (September 21) can support classroom goals of promoting peace and nonviolence. Similarly, Susan B. Anthony's birthday on February 15 provides an opportunity to highlight strong girls and women and changing things that aren't fair, two other possible program goals.

Holidays that commemorate social justice

Holidays that commemorate struggles for justice, peace, and freedom offer children examples of people who worked hard to correct unfair situations. Celebrating these holidays can lead to discussions about what children can do when things are unfair in their lives and about adult leaders who are working for justice today. The Fourth of July, which celebrates the adoption of the Declaration of Independence, and Martin Luther King Jr.'s birthday (January 15, but celebrated as a federal holiday on the third Monday in January), which celebrates one important man in the struggle for civil rights, are two examples of these holidays.

Holidays to broaden children's perspectives

If one of your goals for holidays is to stretch children's awareness, empathy, and understanding of similarities and differences, but the children in your program celebrate the same holidays in similar ways, you might consider introducing holidays that no one in the classroom celebrates at home. If your children are at least three years old, introducing these holidays can help them understand that people celebrate different holidays in various ways and that all of them are valid. On the other hand, introducing unfamiliar cultural holidays easily leads to a tourist approach that undermines your goals of teaching empathy and understanding. Deciding whether or not to introduce these holidays requires a lot of thought. See chapter 11, "Introduce Unfamiliar Holidays," for information and ideas.

Caution

Even if your children all celebrate the same holidays, you can teach about similarities and differences by focusing on the wide variations in the ways people celebrate. Don't feel as if you must expose children to unfamiliar cultural holidays to accomplish this goal. In fact, it may be preferable not to.

Holidays that provide opportunities for critical thinking

Some holidays children are exposed to every year contain stereotypes or perpetuate misinformation about a historical event or group of people. Depending on the ages of the children in your classroom, you might include some of these holidays as strategies for directly addressing the stereotypes children are exposed to and promoting critical thinking. For example, Thanksgiving can be one of the times you discuss stereotypes about American Indians, and at Halloween you can talk about stereotypes of older women and the color black. Many holidays have also become highly commercialized in our society. Discussing that issue with children around Christmas, Halloween, Thanksgiving, Valentine's Day, or Easter, for example, is another way to help children become critical thinkers and help them resist the impact of consumerism. Chapter 5, "Address Stereotypes and Commercialism," discusses these issues and offers strategies for addressing them.

Classroom culture holidays

You might have invented holidays that you celebrate every year and that have become a part of your classroom culture. These should also be included on your list. They may not be special to any other group of children in any other program, but they have particular meaning and relevance for your group. And they are a wonderful way to build connections and a sense of community among children and teachers in your room. Just a few of the many invented holidays used in classrooms are Backwards Day, when regular classroom practices and routines are reversed; Tea Party celebrations, when children bring in their favorite dolls or teddy bears for a tea party; and Wheel Day, when children and adults bring to school a bike, skateboard, wagon, roller skates, or other wheeled toy to ride during outside time. If your program does special birthday celebrations for children or end-of-the-year events such as graduation ceremonies, these can be considered invented holidays as well.

Community holidays

Some programs include holiday celebrations that are of special local importance. For example, in Joseph, Oregon, a small town north of Portland, many schools and child care programs celebrate Chief Joseph Day because their town is named after this important peace activist. Other communities may have a clambake, a tulip festival, or other days to celebrate.

Current events

Important events that children will be exposed to during the year may influence your holiday decisions. Election Day, when the country votes on a new president, is one example. Similarly, if the country is in the midst of a war, then Veterans Day may be a holiday to include on your list.

EVALUATE YOUR LIST

At this point, you'll need to go back and assess how you are doing in selecting holidays. Keep in mind that the holidays in your classroom will probably differ from those in the classroom next door or down the hall. This is a good sign! It means that you are including holidays that meet the specific needs of the children and families in your classroom.

The holiday goals you decided on in chapter 8 should be your overriding guidelines when choosing holidays now. Take time to go over each holiday on your current list and be clear about how it relates to your selected goals. Make sure that you haven't kept any holidays on your list just because you've always included them. When you are done, consider asking families for their responses to your final list. Verify that their important days are represented, and find out if they are uncomfortable with any of the holidays included.

You may find that you now have too many holidays and need to pare down your list. The following strategies can help you in your evaluation.

Set a standard

You may find it helpful to decide on a number of goals a holiday must meet to be included in your program. This is especially useful if you are trying to limit the number of holidays on your list. Two or three goals are a good baseline.

Prioritize goals according to your group

Try to identify which goals are the most important for the group of children and families you work with. For example, if your children are all European American, the main goals may focus on connections, becoming aware of the diversity in how different European American families celebrate, exploring holidays that are celebrated in the community but not in the program, and helping children realize that theirs isn't the only or "right" way to celebrate. If your children are all children of color and they celebrate some holidays that aren't commonly represented outside of their homes, one of the most important goals might be to validate what the children and families celebrate in order to nurture positive self-esteem and group identities. Creating opportunities for connections would also be an important goal. With a very diverse group of children of color and European American children, your main goals might focus on validating each child and expanding on the many similarities and differences among them.

Consider religion

Be aware of the strong religious components that are part of many holidays. If teaching about religion is not a goal for you or is not appropriate to your setting, decide if you will be able to include the holiday while avoiding this aspect (see "Consider Religion," chapter 4, for information and strategies).

Remember your bottom line

No matter how many goals a holiday activity may meet, if including it hurts a single child or family in any way, or teaches hurtful information, consider carefully whether you will continue to include this activity in the curriculum. For example, children may enjoy wearing Indian headdresses and acting out the first Thanksgiving, but that practice can severely hurt American Indian children in the classroom and other children's growing sense of who American Indian people are. Similarly, celebrating Cinco de Mayo may seem like a good way to celebrate similarities and differences, but if no one in the classroom or community celebrates it, and it is the only activity about Mexican Americans that you celebrate, then it becomes a tourist activity, and you should avoid it.

CHAPTER 11

Introduce Unfamiliar Holidays

Using holidays as a primary means for teaching children about unfamiliar cultures is a popular but seriously flawed practice. Often the result is activities that can trivialize and stereotype cultural groups and that have no connection to children's lives. Louise Derman-Sparks has described these as tourist activities (Derman-Sparks and the ABC Task Force 1989). Still, there are potential benefits to introducing children to cultural groups they are not familiar with, and holidays can be part of your overall approach. Before you plan activities around holidays that no one in your group celebrates, though, it's important to think about if this makes sense for your children.

STRENGTHEN CHILDREN BY INCLUDING UNFAMILIAR HOLIDAYS

There are a few good reasons to introduce children to holidays that no one in your program celebrates at home. One is to help children become a bit less egocentric and more accepting of holiday practices that differ from their own. Young children tend to think that everyone does the same things they do and that their way is the only right way. For children who celebrate majority holidays, this perspective can be compounded by decorations, songs, books, movies, and television programs that reinforce the way certain holidays are celebrated at home. It is wonderful for children to feel pride in and attachment to their family rituals; however, there is also value in helping them learn that many people celebrate holidays that are different from but just as important as their own.

Another reason to introduce unfamiliar holidays is to help prepare children for the world of diversity that they will undoubtedly encounter as they grow.

Reinforcing the concept of similarities and differences in as many ways as possible while children are young helps them develop the necessary skills and feelings (such as comfort and empathy) that enable them to interact comfortably with the many different people they will meet and experience as adults.

In many cases, however, young children may not be able to learn these skills from holiday activities, because the activities are too complex or too removed from their daily lives. So how or when do you know whether to include these holidays in your classroom?

CONSIDER CHILDREN'S DEVELOPMENT

The first factor to keep in mind is the developmental stages of the children you teach. Refer back to Holiday Ages and Stages in chapter 2, pages 35–38, to review how children experience holidays at different ages. Some theorists tell us that there seems to be a developmental shift for children around the ages of five to seven years, when they begin to have a wider and more flexible understanding of different people and different rituals. Because their minds can handle a little more abstract thinking at these ages, they become receptive to concepts that are more complex than those they grappled with in their preschool years. For example, third graders can begin to talk about people in other countries, what they wear when celebrating, and what they wear when playing with their friends. They are able to compare and contrast the practices of people in other countries with what they do in their own houses.

What you can expect to introduce to four-year-old children will be very different from what a primary classroom teacher can successfully introduce. Four-year-olds do not have the ability to think abstractly and reason in the ways of older children. Without some direct experience of the lives of people who live in other countries, preschool children can't comprehend who these people are or how their lives are similar to or different from their own. They need concrete, firsthand experiences in order to learn and understand.

CONSIDER THE COMMUNITY CONTEXT

While keeping in mind the ages and developmental stages of children in your program, also consider the types of communities in which they live. Young children need holiday activities that are similar in some way to their own lives and beliefs, or those of people they know. Any holiday activity you share with the children must be connected to their own experiences in some way.

Do your children live in a racially, ethnically, or culturally diverse community with a lot of exposure to children and families whose beliefs and practices are different from their own? Or do they live in a mostly homogeneous area, where virtually everyone celebrates the same way they do? Considering these questions will help you determine the number of unfamiliar cultural holidays, if any, and how much about a given holiday you can successfully introduce.

If your children live in a diverse area, they will have more concrete experiences with different people to draw on. They are far more likely to have been exposed to various holidays, even if they don't celebrate them. Perhaps the Mexican restaurant next door decorates for Cinco de Mayo, or the mall down the street has a Kwanzaa celebration. In these communities, children often play with neighbors who celebrate differently from themselves, or they encounter other children's holidays while interacting in playgroups, dance classes, library story times, and so on. As a result, you can introduce a variety of holidays, because you can more easily create connections to children's own lives.

You will be more limited in how much you can do with unfamiliar cultural holidays if your children live in a homogeneous community where everyone comes from a similar background and celebrates as they do, and if there is little opportunity for them to encounter diversity in other areas of their lives. In some ways, children living in these contexts have a greater need to be exposed to diversity, but teachers have fewer resources to help create connections and firsthand experiences for these children. Therefore, when you consider using holidays to accomplish this goal, the likelihood of your falling into the trap of a tourist approach increases. You will always have more success introducing unfamiliar holidays with older children (five years and above) than with younger ones.

Diversity in Homogeneous Groups

If the children in your group have little exposure to diversity, your best choice may be to use methods other than holiday activities to broaden their perspective and reinforce the concept of similarities and differences. Here are a few ideas and resources.

Use the Diversity That You Have

There will be differences in any group of children (or adults), even in seemingly homogeneous groups. Children will look somewhat different, live in a variety of homes, have different family configurations, like to do different things, and celebrate the same holidays differently. Build discussions and activities around these aspects of their lives to talk about similarities and differences. A multitude of children's books are available now that address similarities and differences in skin, hair, family structures, homes, and so much more.

Read Children's Literature

Look for stories with protagonists who are different from your group in appearance or family structure (for example, those who have physical disabilities, darker skin, or live in gay- or lesbian-headed families) but encounter familiar, everyday situations (such as the first day of school or going to the doctor).

> ### Introduce Children to Persona Dolls
>
> Use persona dolls that have different cultural and ethnic backgrounds to tell your group stories about their experiences that your children can relate to. Some of the stories might be about a holiday celebration they had at their "homes" (see Use Persona Dolls, page 127, for more information).

USE A DIAGRAM TO HELP YOU DECIDE

On pages 124 and 125, I offer you two diagrams made up of concentric circles. These tools can be used to help you decide if you should include unfamiliar holidays. If you go ahead, they can help you decide which unfamiliar holidays to include, based on your children's experiences with diversity. The diagrams illustrate a child's realm of experiences and exposures. The child is in the center, and her environment radiates out. The people or experiences most familiar to the child are closest, and the people or experiences most unfamiliar are farthest away.

There will be different concentric circle diagrams for different programs, depending on many factors—for example, if children were born in the United States or another country, or if they live in a rural, isolated area or a central, urban area. The following examples are completed diagrams for children in two sample classrooms. Diagram A on page 124 reflects children whose families have been in the United States for three or four generations. They have limited experiences out of their state and very little out of the country. Diagram B on page 125 represents a different population of children. These children were born in Guatemala, Korea, and Mexico, and are newly arrived in America. Their experiences in other countries are still more familiar to them than those in the United States. Depending on how successful the teachers in their program have been at including elements of the children's daily lives in the classroom, and whether the communities that the children live in reflect their ethnic and cultural lives, the layer outside of "other countries" will be either school/center or neighborhood/community. Similarly, if a child regularly visits one of her parents in another state, that state will be familiar and will appear closer to the center.

To make your own diagram, think about your children's experiences. Start from the middle and move out, filling in circles with the names of people or places that children are most familiar with and ending with those that are least familiar. You may need to complete more than one diagram if your children come from different types of backgrounds or live in different kinds of communities.

When your diagram or diagrams are complete, review them in light of your children's ages. This will tell you what kinds of holidays they will be able to connect to. As a rule of thumb, if your children are two years old, they need activities that relate to layers 1, 2, or 3. Threes and fours probably won't gain much from activities outside layer 4 or 5. Fives may benefit from activities up to and including layer 6, depending on their experiences. Six-, seven-, and eight-year-olds might enjoy activities that reach out into layer 7 or so.

The diagrams will help you think about how much and what kinds of diversity children are exposed to in their daily lives. This information will help you decide if you should introduce unfamiliar holidays, which holidays those might be, and how much material about that holiday would be appropriate to introduce in your curriculum.

Are children's own families diverse? For example, do they live in interracial families, or have two moms or two dads, or was their grandmother born in another country? How diverse is their school or child care program? Are there children from different backgrounds, and are various languages spoken and/or a variety of religions observed? How about the diversity of the community children live in? What do the store owners and workers in their neighborhood look like? What languages do they speak? For older children, you can also think about the level of diversity that exists in the outer layers of their circle.

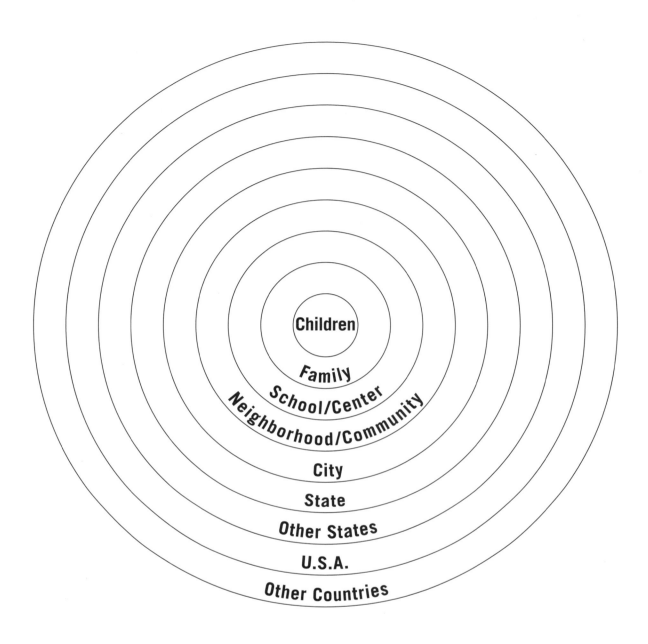

Diagram A

Children whose families have lived in the United States for three or four generations

Diagram B

Children who have recently moved to the United States

INCLUDE UNFAMILIAR HOLIDAYS

If you decide that your children are ready to learn about holidays with which they have no direct experience, you must make the connections for them between the holiday and the people or experiences that are already familiar to them. This way you provide valuable opportunities for exploring similarities and differences without using a tourist approach to diversity. Here are some strategies that other educators have used for making successful connections.

Allow learning about a holiday to emerge naturally

When children are acquainted with individuals from a cultural group other than their own, or older children learn a lot about the members of a specific cultural group, the holiday practices of the group emerge naturally. Teachers don't have to force them. The following is an example.

Teddy Bear Head Start has four- and five-year-old children from a variety of cultures, including El Salvadorian, Mexican, Japanese, Korean, European American, American Indian, and African American. There are no Chinese American children in the program, and no one celebrates Chinese New Year. However, the program is situated in a diverse inner-city neighborhood that includes a substantial Chinese American population. Some of the children in the program play with neighbors and friends who are Chinese. Their older siblings attend school with children who are Chinese American.

Every year in this community there is a huge Chinese New Year celebration, including a parade that passes in front of Teddy Bear Head Start. Learning about Chinese New Year in the classroom seems natural, because it is an important holiday in the community where the program is located and where many children live, and the children have some understanding of who Chinese people are. Teachers can introduce the holiday in a meaningful way because they know that their discussions about this holiday won't be the first time children learn anything about people who are Chinese or Chinese American.

Talk to a class friend

If there is someone who regularly visits your classroom and who celebrates a holiday that is new to children, invite that person to share it with the group. The visitor might be a librarian, public health nurse, teacher trainer, custodian, diaper delivery person, Spanish teacher, or supervisor or director. It is important for children to know the person well before he is asked to speak about a holiday. The children need to connect to the individual first before they can connect to the person's holiday in a meaningful way (Sharon Cronin, interview with author, April 1992).

Share your own holidays

If you celebrate a holiday that your children do not, your explanation of the holiday and how you experience it provides a concrete way for children to understand it. Sharing this part of yourself will also allow the children to connect with you in a new, more personal way.

Use persona dolls

One of the most effective ways to tell stories to children is through persona dolls, whose physical characteristics can include any of a variety of skin colors and features. Some persona dolls also have physical disabilities. In the classroom, these dolls have distinct personas that never change. The dolls come out at various times, and the children eventually learn all about them, as if they are additional members of the classroom. The children also learn about each doll's special holidays as they come up, just as they would with anyone else in the classroom.

For example, Katherine is a persona doll with light brown skin, long, light brown hair, and almond-shaped eyes. Her mother is European American and her father is Japanese American. Katherine's grandfather, who is ill, lives at her house and has a nurse who takes care of him during the day while her parents work. Katherine visits the classroom on many occasions so her teacher can tell a story about something that happened to her that is very similar to something that happened to a child in the class. Sometimes these are everyday stories, such as helping children solve an issue that arises in the sandbox. Sometimes it is a more personal story about Katherine's feelings or experiences at home. The beauty of persona dolls is that you can supplement what actually happens in the classroom through the experiences of the dolls. Below is an example of a persona doll who shares an unfamiliar holiday with the children in one teacher's classroom.

Sample Persona Doll Story: "Thomas Celebrates Solstice"

When I brought a persona doll named Thomas to circle time in the preschool room, the children welcomed their friend to the group with enthusiasm. Several children yelled, "Yay! Thomas is here!" Thomas had visited the children a few times prior. The visit they remember the most was when he came to the group with Lauren, another doll, because the two of them had a problem. Thomas always wanted to play with Lauren, just Lauren and no one else. Lauren liked Thomas but was annoyed that he always followed her around and wanted to play with only her. I brought the dolls and the problem to the group because a similar, real-life situation was happening in the preschool room. I presented the problem and asked the children to brainstorm ways that Lauren and Thomas could solve it. This time, however, I brought Thomas to the group on December 21 to tell the children about how Thomas celebrates Solstice. I began the story . . .

"Thomas came to visit you today because he wants to tell you about a special holiday that he celebrates with his family. We've been talking a lot about holidays lately. Last week, we talked about Hanukkah and how some of you celebrate Hanukkah at your homes, and now we're talking about Christmas. There are other holidays at this time of the year, and one of them is called Solstice. This is a holiday that Thomas celebrates at his house. He brought a special book with him today that he wants me to read to you about Solstice. The book is called Dear Rebecca, Winter Is Here.*"*

Then I read the book, which simply and concretely talks about the changes in the seasons. After I finished reading the book, I explained a little bit more about Solstice.

"Solstice is a time of year when some people celebrate the fact that the days are getting longer and the sun is starting to stay out longer. Remember when the days started getting shorter and it started getting dark right after snacktime, before your moms or dads picked you up? Well, soon after Solstice, the days will start getting longer again, and soon it will be light out when your moms and dads pick you up. Some people think this is very important and like to celebrate it. At Thomas's house, they celebrate Solstice by decorating a tree outside in their front yard with food for the birds and squirrels. They hang up peanut butter birdfeeders, popcorn string, and other treats that animals like. They also light candles in their house to celebrate the sun and the light that starts to come back after Solstice."

After this discussion, I explained to the children that Thomas was inviting them to make candleholders with him today in honor of Solstice. After circle time, the children joined Thomas at the art table and had a great time molding and decorating clay candleholders for the candles they chose.

Connect unfamiliar holidays to familiar ones

One way to make the connection between unfamiliar holidays and children's own lives is to focus on the underlying themes that many holidays have in common, such as festivals of light or liberation. Children are able to identify more successfully with a holiday and the people who celebrate it when the new celebration has a theme similar to that of their own holiday. Here are some examples of common themes and a sampling of holidays associated with them:

★ **Liberation:** Fourth of July, Mexican Independence Day, Passover, Hanukkah, Cinco de Mayo, Juneteenth (June 19, 1865, the day when slaves in Texas learned they were free), and Martin Luther King Jr.'s birthday

- **Harvest:** Thanksgiving, Kwanzaa, Sukkot (Jewish harvest festival), Makahiki (Hawaiian harvest)

- **New Year:** American New Year's Day, Rosh Hashanah (Jewish New Year), Chinese New Year, Hmong New Year, Têt (Vietnamese New Year) (Note that almost all cultures have a new year celebration. This is just a sampling.)

- **Death:** Día de los Muertos (Mexican Day of the Dead), Kwanzaa, All Souls' Day, Memorial Day

- **Festivals of Light:** Christmas, Hanukkah, Kwanzaa, Santa Lucia Day (Swedish light festival), Diwali (Hindu festival of lights), Solstice

There are many ways to make the connections among holidays for children. One way is simply to explain the connection in age-appropriate language. You might say, "Remember when we talked about the holiday called the Fourth of July? Remember that we talked about it being a liberation celebration because it was the birth of the United States? Well, we're going to talk about another holiday that is a liberation celebration, and that is called Hanukkah. Some people who are Jewish celebrate Hanukkah because it reminds them of a long time ago when Jewish people fought to take something back that was theirs. They fought to take back their temple, which had been taken away from them" (ReGena Booze, interview with author, April 1992).

The festival of light theme can then be exemplified in activities that celebrate light. For example, teachers at the child care program at Pacific Oaks Children's School in Pasadena, California, have invented a candle group ritual that takes place during the winter months, when the days get shorter and the October, November, December, and January holidays emerge. The children make candleholders to hold their own special candles, and every day at around 5:30 p.m., half an hour before the center closes for the day, the children all gather on the carpet for Candle Group. The safety rules about candles are reviewed, the candles are lit, and the lights are dimmed. Children are invited to sing peaceful songs related to the holidays, the time of the year, liberation struggles, or anything else that comes to mind. They know that this is a special ritual saved for the time of the year when the days grow shorter and when the holidays that relate to light (Solstice, Kwanzaa, Hanukkah, Christmas, Diwali, Santa Lucia Day, and others) are around the corner.

Weave aspects of different holidays into your program year-round

Keep holiday books on the book shelves all year so children and teachers can have conversations anytime about particular holidays and the values they represent. Let relevant decorations stay up on the walls. For example, good luck symbols from Chinese New Year and a poster of the Nguzo Saba (Seven Principles of Kwanzaa) commemorate principles that can be incorporated into the curriculum all year. Through repetition and connection to daily events, the holidays and the meanings that underlie them become more familiar.

Here's an example of how this works. The seven principles of Kwanzaa are Umoja (unity), Kujichagulia (self-determination), Ujima (working together), Ujamaa (cooperative economics), Nia (purpose), Kuumba (creativity), and Imani (faith). You might choose to make the principles of working together, creativity, and faith (having confidence in ourselves) year-round themes in your classroom, well before the holiday begins. As you talk about these principles, they will come to have meaning for your children, and in turn, the holiday that celebrates them will become more meaningful. When Kwanzaa comes around in December, you can remind children that you've been talking about the important messages of the Nguzo Saba all year long (ReGena Booze, interview with author, April 1992).

Points to Remember

Whatever strategies you use for introducing unfamiliar cultural holidays, keep these important points in mind:

- ★ Activities about a holiday should never be children's first introduction to or last mention of a cultural group. Children must first have an understanding of who people are and how they live their daily lives so they can build a context in which to comprehend a holiday or celebration. Without this context, information about a holiday may seem too different from their own experience and too difficult to understand. As a result, children may form stereotypes about the "strange" people who celebrate this "different" holiday.

- ★ Focus on the feelings people have when they celebrate their special holiday or engage in a family ritual. Feelings are real for young children and something they can connect to and identify with, especially if the feeling is related to one they've had before. Be careful not to focus on external pieces of a holiday, such as food or dress, without including the feeling component.

- ★ When you introduce activities from other people's holidays, you run the risk of doing them inappropriately. Make sure you do your research and gather sufficient information about the holiday so that you don't give children any misinformation or perpetuate stereotypes. A visit to the communities of people who celebrate the holiday can offer you a lot of information. You can also use the library, children's books, individuals in the community, and cultural centers for information.

Deciding if and how to include unfamiliar holidays in your classroom is an important piece of implementing an anti-bias approach to holidays. The issues may seem complicated, but with planning, forethought, and ongoing reflection and evaluation, you will make the best decisions for your program.

CHAPTER 12

Assess Your Holiday Activities

Celebrate! began with my descriptions of how holidays work—and don't—in preschool classrooms. The second and third parts of *Celebrate!* have offered you practical advice on how to partner with children's families, coworkers, and administrators to clarify how, when, which, and how often holidays will be included in your curriculum. Once you have assessed your situation, begun a holiday policy, and decided on your goals for holiday activities and the holidays you will include, you will be ready to begin with a new approach in the classroom.

Now let's focus on the final step in the process of change: assessing your holiday activities. When you regularly reflect on and evaluate your activities, you are ensuring that they continue to meet the needs of the children and to accomplish what you intend. Evaluating and reevaluating practices gives you opportunities to improve. Eventually, you will develop the practices that accomplish your goals and meet the changing needs of children and families. Follow these steps to guide you in your efforts.

MEET TO REVIEW YOUR ACTIVITIES

Set aside time shortly after each holiday to sit down with other staff members, and parents and guardians if possible, to talk about what worked and what didn't in your activities. Ask yourselves the following questions:

* Did we include this holiday for good reasons? How were families involved in making the decision?

* How were families involved in planning and implementing the holiday activities?

- Are we satisfied with the amount of knowledge we had about this holiday? Did we have adequate materials?

- How well did the holiday activities we included and the discussions we had with children meet our goals for holidays?

- Did we portray this holiday in relevant ways for the children and families in the program who celebrate it?

- How authentically did we portray the story behind this holiday? What input did we get to determine this?

- How did families respond to the way we handled this holiday? What feedback, if any, did we get from them?

If the holiday you are reviewing was one that neither you nor the children in the program celebrate, ask yourselves these additional questions:

- If I were a member of the group that celebrates this holiday, how would I feel about this representation of me and my holiday?

- If this were the first time I had heard about this holiday, what is one thing I would gain from this experience?

- Did we introduce this holiday using connections that we and the children have made with people who celebrate it as part of their culture or religion?

- Did we pass on any misinformation?

- Did we successfully avoid making this holiday seem exotic?

PLAN FOR IMPROVEMENT

Agree together on a plan for improving your approach. Try using the questions on the next page or another tool that meets your needs. Remember that the first time you try out an activity, you may not be entirely satisfied with it. With more experience, information, feedback, and planning, your practices will get better. Keep at it!

Holiday Practices Improvement Plan

What went really well?

What could be improved?

What changes will we make next time?

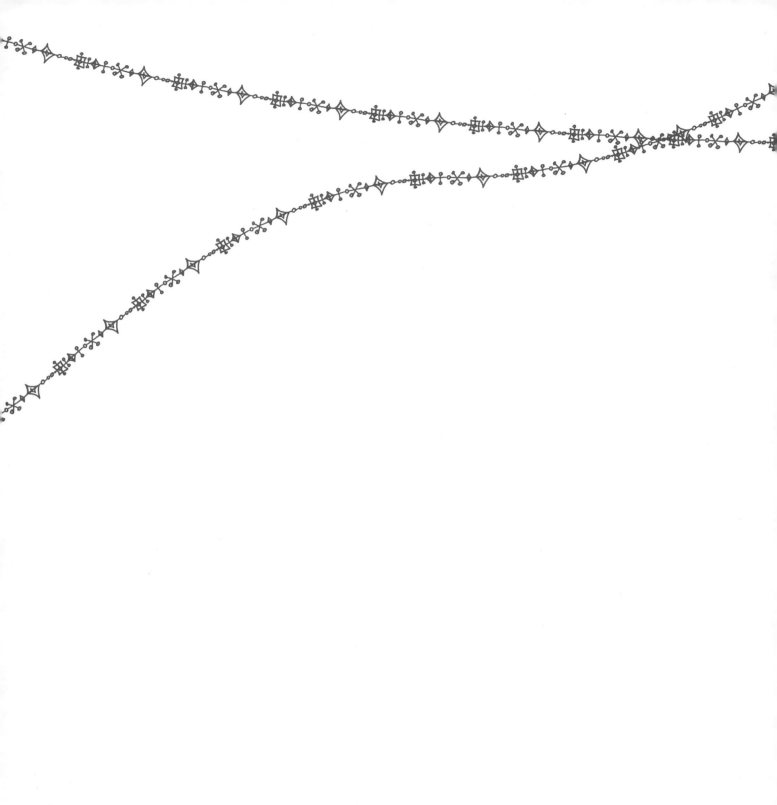

....

CHAPTER 13

Putting It All Together: Holidays in Three Classrooms

While all early childhood teachers will take similar steps to define their approach to holidays, holiday practices will ultimately vary widely from program to program. This chapter offers three stories set in three different early childhood settings. The stories are told from the perspective of the teachers who work in the program and describe the children and families who make up the program and how each program handles holidays. The teachers and the names of the programs are fictitious, but the holiday practices described are ones used in real-life programs.

Michael's Story

Michael teaches three-year-olds in a classroom at Dandelion Child Care Center. This center is a private, nonprofit, nonsectarian child care program that serves children ages two months to five years. It is entirely funded by tuition.

The children who attend Dandelion are mostly European American, with a few African American and a few Asian American children. Almost all of the children come from middle- to upper-middle-income families, except for a few children whose tuition is subsidized by the city. A variety of religious beliefs are represented, including Christian, Jewish, and Muslim. Some of the families are also Jehovah's Witnesses.

Approach to holidays

Holidays are a fairly significant part of the program. I include about two or three holidays in the curriculum each month.

Goals

I make sure that the holidays of the children in the program have a prominent place in the curriculum. I feel it is imperative to validate the children's and families' identities and beliefs and to recognize that what they do at home together is very important to them. At the same time, I know that for the Christian children, whose holidays are represented everywhere in the media, stores, cards, and decorations, it is particularly valuable to learn that there are other holidays celebrated in the world that are just as valid and important as those that they celebrate.

Choosing holidays

I put together a list of holidays, starting with what children and families in the program celebrate, as well as what I celebrate. I learn about what and how families celebrate by sending out questionnaires. I include the holidays that I celebrate personally because this is a natural extension of the children's relationship with me. They spend five days with me every week. Learning about the days and events that are important to me is something they are interested in. I think it makes me seem more regular to them, especially when what I celebrate or the way I do it is similar to their practices. Then I include a few other holidays because I really want to expand awareness of and comfort with differences among this fairly homogeneous group. To make sure children have some real-life connection with these holidays, I choose ones that are celebrated in the surrounding community.

This year the holidays that the children and families in the program celebrate are the American New Year, Martin Luther King Jr.'s birthday, Chinese New Year, Valentine's Day, St. Patrick's Day, Easter, Passover, Fourth of July, Rosh Hashanah, Halloween, Ramadan, Eid al-Fitr—which celebrates the end of the fasting during Ramadan—Thanksgiving, Hanukkah, Christmas, and Mother's and Father's Days. We celebrate these last two as "Family Day" because that is more inclusive and respects the different family configurations we have in our program. One of the holidays I celebrate that I will share with the children is Solstice. The community holidays I'll bring in include Día de Los Muertos (Day of the Dead) and Kwanzaa.

Implementation

Holiday activities in our classroom can be as simple as reading a book about a holiday and as elaborate and involved as having a party in the classroom, with food, decorations, guests, and music. In most cases, however, holidays are more recognized than celebrated. Our activities usually involve a short group discussion about a holiday and how a family celebrates it, or we'll read a book about a holiday.

Occasionally I will set up developmentally appropriate activities for children that relate to a holiday. These activities are usually centered on the way a family in the program celebrates at home. For example, in October and November many of the children in my classroom have pumpkins in their homes, so we often experiment with pumpkins during that time. I cut open a pumpkin and put it in the sensory table so children can touch the flesh, feel the coolness inside, separate the seeds from the pumpkin, and experience the smell of fresh pumpkin. Later we rinse and dry the seeds and bake them, like many children have done or will do at home. Sometimes family members will come in and take part in an activity with us. One year, the children and I designed jack-o'-lantern faces, and I helped a parent cut them out.

Although less common, we occasionally have a party to celebrate a holiday. This usually happens when families really want a party. For example, if some children's older siblings are having a Halloween or Valentine's Day party in grade school, families sometimes want their preschoolers to have one too. The family members do the planning. They will bring in a special treat and maybe some napkins and paper cups, and we'll sing and have a little party. I just ask them to keep it fairly low key so the children don't get overstimulated.

Because of the age group of the children in my classroom, oftentimes I talk about holidays after they've occurred instead of before. The holidays are fresher in children's minds then and the discussions are more meaningful to them. I've tried to ask children what their family did for a particular holiday last year, and generally they just don't remember. But when we come back to school on January 2, after a short winter break, some of the children want to talk about how they had a New Year party at their house and Grandma or Auntie came over for dinner.

I often tie holidays together by their common themes. I've found that this works really well for my three-year-olds, who need to hear the same concepts repeated over and over again. I use this approach to introduce holidays that are present in the community but not celebrated by families in the classroom. For example, many children in the program celebrate Christmas and Hanukkah. We talk about the common theme of light in both holidays; there are lights on the Christmas tree, lights on the advent wreath, lights on the menorah. This paves the way for understanding something about Kwanzaa and Solstice, because there are lights on the Kwanzaa kinara, and Solstice is all about the return of light (the sun) as the days get longer again. Throughout this time, we experiment with flashlights, make candleholders out of clay, and eat lunch and nap by candlelight. One day last year, a parent brought in a menorah and I brought in a kinara (candleholder for Kwanzaa), and we lit both during naptime. The older threes have really latched onto this idea of Christmas, Hanukkah, Solstice, and Kwanzaa all being festivals of light. I can point out that while they are celebrating Christmas, Hanukkah, or both, other people are celebrating Kwanzaa or Solstice, holidays that are similar to but different from theirs.

Religion

Since Dandelion is a private program, we have lots of leeway with religion. In my classroom, I have chosen to actively tell the religious stories that go with holidays. The director is very supportive of this approach. Of course, this has to be done very simply with threes, and I am very careful to give concrete, non-biased information. I use the words *some people* when I talk about religion so that children begin to learn that not everyone believes in the same religious stories or the same religion. For example, I will say, "Some people, people who are Christians, believe in Jesus. On Christmas, people who believe in Jesus celebrate his birthday because they are so happy he was born." Then, to make it concrete for children, I'll say, "At Sally's house, this is what they believe, and they go to church on Christmas to celebrate Jesus's birthday." Similarly, to explain Ramadan, I tell children that people who are Muslim celebrate this day to remember their God, Allah, and his follower, Muhammad. I also explain that during Ramadan, adults and some children fast (that means they eat only after the sun goes down and before it comes up in the morning). I work very closely with families on the issue of religion. I explain to them ahead of time how I will talk about the religious aspects of holidays and give them time to give me feedback. I always refer children back to their parents if they ask for more information.

Working with families

In our school, families are fairly involved. We have bimonthly family meetings on a variety of topics and a policy that requires family members to participate in the program in some way at least one hour every month. I also communicate with parents and guardians regularly, especially at the end of the day, about their children and how the day was.

At the beginning of each year, I send out questionnaires asking for a lot of information, including information about holidays. Then I invite families to a meeting on this topic. I describe how I tend to handle holidays, and I invite family members to help make decisions about what and how we'll celebrate during the coming year. We'll talk about developmentally appropriate practices and the need to tailor all activities to the developmental levels of three-year-olds. I remind families that at this age, children will need lots of hands-on activities that stimulate their senses. They will relate the most to short books, short discussions, and activities from their own and others' homes. I'll also take the opportunity at a meeting to ask families for information about their own holidays, especially if I haven't yet gotten back their questionnaires. Then I get together with parents and guardians on a regular basis, at least once a year, to assess how our holiday practices have been working and where we can improve.

Throughout the process, I work to build trust with families. I want them to be involved with this part of the curriculum as much as possible. I also want to involve families in my efforts to make sure there is equality among the holidays presented.

Working with children who don't celebrate

I do have two families in the classroom who are Jehovah's Witnesses and don't celebrate holidays. This has been a real challenge for me, but one that I've welcomed. I've used it as a series of teachable moments, another way to talk about differences and similarities. One of the families tends to be flexible about what their daughter can participate in. She is able to be present in the classroom when we are discussing a holiday, because we are usually just reading a book or talking about it. I always make sure to tell her mom about every single activity I am planning so she has some time to talk with me about it before it happens. Many times, the child can participate in the activities I plan because I present them in a way that is acceptable to her mother. For example, I always set up all of my activities as a choice so no one, including this child, ever has to participate if she doesn't want to. She can just choose one of the other activities.

The other family in my classroom seems to be stricter. Whenever we are doing an actual holiday-related activity, the child and I, and any other children who want to, leave the room. For example, in the fall a parent came in to cut out jack-o'-lanterns with the children. Before they got started, I went for a walk to the library with the child who couldn't participate, and Amy, my assistant, stayed in the classroom with the director. On the way to the library, I explained to the child that her mom and dad thought it might be too hard for her to be in the classroom right now because some kids are cutting out jack-o'-lanterns and her parents don't want her to. While we're gone, Amy explains to the other children why this child left the room. She uses this opportunity to teach about religious diversity. Amy will say something to the children like "Some families believe in making jack-o'-lanterns and some don't. It depends on your religious beliefs and what your family wants you to do." In general, the parents of this child have been pleased with our efforts to meet their needs and not ostracize them or their child. I am careful not to disapprove of them, and I do not treat them like they are depriving their child because they don't celebrate birthdays or holidays.

Sheryl's Story

Sheryl teaches four- and five-year-olds in a classroom at Spruce Street Head Start. As a Head Start program, Spruce Street is public, nonsectarian, and receives its funding from the federal government.

The children who go to Spruce Street are from many racial and ethnic backgrounds, including Latino (El Salvadorian, Guatemalan, Mexican), African American, Asian American (Chinese American, Japanese American, Korean American), a small population of American Indians (Anishinaabe/Ojibwe, and a few who are

European American. The majority of the families are Christian, although there are some Muslim, Hindu, and Buddhist families as well. All the children come from low-income families.

Approach to holidays

Holidays are a consistent part of the curriculum but a small part. We don't have many parties, but we do some activities and have discussions. I often use holidays to highlight classroom themes.

Goals

My biggest goal is to validate the children's and families' experiences. Many of the children in my classroom celebrate holidays that they don't see reflected in society at large, so I want them to see them here. Since parents and guardians are involved in Head Start, when they bring in holiday recipes or books or decorations, it helps to make that home/school connection. I also want children to learn about one another's holidays, and I want them to recognize unfairness and take action to change it when they can.

Choosing holidays

I talk about most of the holidays that are celebrated by children and families in the program, even if they are religious. I just try not to focus on the religious aspects. I tend not to talk about any holidays that the families in the classroom don't celebrate, because there is already so much diversity here. I can easily meet my goal of exposing children to holidays other than their own without bringing in any additional holidays.

Holidays that are included this year are Las Posadas, Christmas, Kwanzaa, Hanukkah, Chinese New Year, Japanese New Year, Korean New Year, Hindu New Year, Martin Luther King Jr.'s birthday, Black History Month, Valentine's Day, Hana Matsuri (Japanese Buddhist Flower Festival), Easter, Ramadan, Anishinaabe Thanksgiving for the Maple Trees, Juneteenth, Mexican Independence Day, Halloween, Día de Los Muertos, and Thanksgiving.

Implementation

I try to pick out the underlying, nonreligious values of holidays and focus on those. For Valentine's Day, we focus on the giving as well as the receiving of valentines. We talk a lot about what it means to be a friend and how you show people that you care about them. We also talk about how great it feels to give cards to people we care about. We usually read a book at circle time about friendship, and then, during activity time, I set out a whole array of materials that children can use to make valentines. I try to steer away from commercial influences and provide open-ended materials that are interesting to children—folded construction paper, doilies, glitter, sequins, beads, buttons, stamps, stickers, and cut-out pictures from magazines that reflect their cultural groups. Children can make whatever they'd like with the materials. If they make a card for a friend or family member, that's great. If they don't, that's okay too. For Martin Luther King Jr.'s birthday, we highlight the conversations about fairness that we have all year long. We talk about it not being fair when someone ruins your block structure, tells you that you can't play, or says you talk funny. I explain to them that Martin Luther King and many other people wanted to make things fairer for everyone. We make signs about fairness, whatever the children want to say, and then march through the school with our signs.

I also look for similar underlying values and messages in holidays to make connections for children. For example, for American New Year, I usually talk a little bit with the children, maybe interview them about what they know about the holiday, and write down their words. Then we will talk a little bit about "out with the old and in with the new." Sometimes we wash babies and clean up the classroom. I talk about the other new year celebrations represented in the classroom too, such as Korean, Japanese, and Hindu New Year. Depending on what the children celebrate at home, I go more into the idea of "cleansing for a new beginning," because that is an important theme of many new year holidays. I point out similarities and differences with other holidays to connect these new year celebrations with ones that children are familiar with. Some of our children are still learning English, so our conversations are usually short and simple. In addition, I tie together Juneteenth, Mexican Independence Day, and Black History Month because they all have similar themes of activism and fighting for fairness.

We talk a lot throughout the year about the issues these holidays bring up, then use the holidays to underscore these important ideas. For example, fairness and changing things that aren't fair is an ongoing topic for us. We talk about how a long time ago, people who were African American were slaves. That meant they worked for white people, doing anything they were told to do. Many people, both African Americans and white people, thought that wasn't fair. We talk about Harriet Tubman, John Brown, Frederick Douglass, the Grimké sisters, and others who helped African Americans become free. When June 19 (Juneteenth) comes along, we talk about how this was the day that African Americans who lived in Texas learned they were free. To give the children a frame of reference, we look at a map together, and I point out how far away Texas is from where they live. Depending on the group of children, I might also talk about how far away June 19 is from the day of the Emancipation Proclamation, January 1, and how the African Americans in Texas had to be slaves for so much longer than other slaves.

Another technique I use is having persona dolls tell stories about holidays. I often tell the stories in small groups to make communication easier. Because the dolls are such a powerful teaching tool, they really get the children's attention and help them connect to the holidays and the people who celebrate them. The dolls also keep the focus off the one or two children who might celebrate a particular holiday so they don't feel too different from everyone else. Sometimes that's a concern of families in my classroom. They don't want their children to feel too different. They want them to feel American and to fit in. I let them know that I will work hard to help their children fit in and feel comfortable but that I also want to celebrate their children's identities and their cultural backgrounds. I'm also teaching the parents and guardians how to use the persona dolls so they can tell stories in their native language.

Religion

Though our curriculum includes religious holidays that the children celebrate, religion can be a challenging issue for us because, as a Head Start, we don't do any religious teaching. Since we receive federal money, we have to abide by the separation of church and state. So in activities and discussions, I avoid the religious aspects as much as possible.

This year we will talk about Las Posadas, but it's going to be hard to avoid religion in this case because traditionally this holiday involves reenacting Joseph and Mary's journey when they look for an inn where Mary can give birth. Children usually take part in the dramatization. I will probably invite a family to talk a little bit about how they celebrate, and leave it at that. If children ask me about who Joseph and Mary are, I'll say something like "If you are Christian, you probably believe that Mary was Jesus's mother and Joseph was Mary's husband."

If children want to know more about a religious belief or story, I'll refer them to their families. I do that regularly when children ask questions about religion. I don't want to just cut them off, because I don't want them to get the message that something is wrong with asking questions or with religion itself. For example, a child once asked me if God was real. I responded by asking, "What do you think?" He didn't answer, so I explained, "Teachers here will not tell you about what is true and what's not true about God. Your family and whatever church, mosque, synagogue, or temple you go to is where you will get that answer." Then I am careful to tell children's families about these conversations so they can address the question as they choose to at home.

Working with families

Families are really involved in Head Start. In fact, they are required to spend a certain amount of time in the classroom. So I always have parents and guardians around when I'm teaching, and there are lots of opportunities to talk. I also do home visits at all of the children's houses. I take that opportunity to ask a lot of questions about what the family celebrates, how they celebrate, and what holidays and rituals are important to them. Instead of just asking, "What do you celebrate?" I ask, "What are the most important times of the year in your family? When do you get together? When do you get together with family members that live far away? Which holidays do you spend the most time preparing for? Which ones do you do the most cooking for?" I get rich information when I ask these questions.

Sometimes I also send out questionnaires that ask for similar information about holidays and how people celebrate. I work hard to make sure that the questionnaires get translated for families who speak languages other than English. If I can't find translators, I won't use a questionnaire, because I really want everyone to be included. I also follow up with families quite a few times to explain why I'm handing out the questionnaires and what I'm looking for. I want families to trust me so they feel comfortable sharing this special information with me.

When I want to include a classroom activity for a holiday celebrated by a particular family, I ask that family for a lot of input and guidance so I am sure to present it in an authentic, respectful way. For example, some of our families celebrate American New Year. For one family, this was a particularly important holiday. I invited her in to share some of her rituals with the children. As a group, we cooked black-eyed peas, because for her family, they are a symbol of good luck for the new year.

I feel lucky that families are so involved in Head Start. It makes my job easier, because families are right there to give input, act as resources, and share ideas. With their help, I'm able to implement holiday activities that build connections between home and school and represent individual families and their rituals and customs.

Margery's Story

Margery teaches kindergarten at St. Thomas School, a private, half-day kindergarten program that is a ministry of the Christian church that houses it. Its stated mission lets it be known that St. Thomas is a Christian program with a Christian curriculum. St. Thomas is funded by family tuition and is subsidized by the church.

The children who currently attend St. Thomas are Christian, mostly European American, and from middle-income families.

Approach to holidays

Holidays are a very important part of the program at St. Thomas. Holiday activities appear in the curriculum almost once a month, sometimes more often. The administrators see holidays as a significant part of our Christian education curriculum component. Since we are a Christian program, families are aware of this when they choose us for their children.

Goals

My goals with holidays are to model the Christian values that are important to us at St. Thomas, such as kindness, caring, forgiveness, compassion, honesty, responsibility, unity, peacefulness, respect, tolerance, and standing against injustice. Other goals are to teach the history of the Christian holidays, to help children learn more about one another, and to have fun. All of these goals are overall classroom goals too. The children and their families all really enjoy the holidays we celebrate.

Choosing holidays

The administration decides which holidays will be included in the curriculum. In general, we include all of the Christian holidays and a few nonsectarian holidays every year. The holidays are Thanksgiving, Advent, Christmas, New Year's, Martin Luther King Jr.'s birthday, Valentine's Day, St. Patrick's Day, Ash Wednesday, Good Friday, Easter, and the Fourth of July. We also talk a little bit about Palm Sunday and Holy Thursday when children bring them up. Many of our children attend church services on those days. We don't celebrate Halloween. The administrators and some of the families object to it because they feel it is anti-Christian. In my classroom, I also mention a few holidays of other religions as they are happening so children know that there are other holidays and that people of different faiths observe them. I won't do any actual celebrating of those holidays, though. We also do Veterans Day as a "no war" day, because that holiday fits into St. Thomas's overall program goals of teaching nonviolence and peaceful problem solving.

Implementation

We do lots of holiday activities in the classroom, especially when I can demonstrate Christian values through them. Here are some examples of Christmas activities that we do in kindergarten. At meeting time, we talk directly about what Christmas is and why Christians observe it. I tell children that it is the time of the year when we celebrate the birth of baby Jesus. I explain that the reason we celebrate Jesus is that he modeled God's love. We talk about the Christmas story, specifically about Mary and Joseph going from inn to inn, looking for a place to stay when Mary was about to give birth to Jesus. Children often want to talk about this story further, so I add wooden manger pieces to the block area that the children can use to talk about, or even act out, the birth of baby Jesus. Some other activities I make available are those that focus on the giving as well as the receiving aspects of Christmas. There are materials for making Christmas ornaments and Christmas cards. I set up an activity area with boxes and wrapping paper, tape, and bows so children can wrap presents. Some children go from area to area and make something for their families or other people they care about. We have a wonderful Christmas family potluck one evening in December, when we share food and then go out to carol for senior citizens. When we are finished singing, we come back to the school for hot chocolate. This is a real connecting time for families and children, who all share a common religion and similar values and enjoy this community experience.

When we celebrate Thanksgiving, we emphasize the underlying value of being thankful to God for all that God provides. We try to avoid the issue of pilgrims and Indians because of all of the stereotypes in that story. We do lots of cooking and baking around that time of the year, though, and families come in quite a bit and share favorite family recipes. On the Wednesday before Thanksgiving, we invite all of the families in for a Harvest Feast, and we taste all of the fruits of our labor and enjoy spending time together.

Religion

At St. Thomas, we actively address the religious aspects of the holidays with the intent of teaching Christian values and beliefs. Many families choose to enroll their children at St. Thomas for this very reason. They are all supportive of this approach. In my kindergarten classroom, I am careful to talk about God and Jesus in developmentally appropriate ways. We help children to see God in the awe and wonder of God's creations, such as the flowers, sunsets, and even worms. We also teach about God through the celebration of the children's lives and their relationships. In addition, we want them to experience God in their building of trust and being cared for in our program. This is how they know God. I am careful to allow children time to process information about God. They ask a lot of questions, and I answer them simply and matter-of-factly. In all of this, I work with families so they are clear about what information their children are receiving or asking for. Then parents and guardians can support that curiosity at home in the ways they decide are best for them.

Working with families

Parents are very involved at St. Thomas. Every year there is a room parent for each room who coordinates parties, fundraisers, and snacks for snacktime. Other parents and guardians take turns bringing in and setting up for snacks. Families also really enjoy being involved in holiday activities at school. This is partly because holidays tend to be a big part of most of their own lives at home, and they enjoy sharing them with their children and with us. In my classroom, I regularly invite families to help with activities. Some families bring in cookies to share or a family recipe so we can make the cookies at school. Other families bring in decorations to put up in the classroom. Still others bring in holiday books to share with the children. I really encourage their participation so they can model for children the fact that there are similarities and differences in the ways that all the families celebrate the same holidays. The families also help me coordinate our Christmas presentation, which we put on right before the winter break. They help make costumes, organize the potluck, and decorate the church basement.

Your holiday activities will not look exactly like any one of these programs. In fact, no two programs should look exactly alike, since no two programs have exactly the same makeup of teachers, children, and families. You may find, however, that your holidays resemble bits and pieces of each of these three classrooms. That's fine. Use these descriptions to help you as you continue to refine your approach, your goals, and your work with families, and to carve out a holiday program that is just right for your setting.

PART FOUR

....

Resources

Appendix A: Further Reading

CHILDREN'S RESOURCES

In the first edition of *Celebrate!* I included a list of children's books about a variety of holidays. My criteria were that they be accurate, sensitive, and reflective of the lives of real people; developmentally appropriate for young children; free of stereotypes; and, overall, good children's literature. Almost exclusively, the people and places in the books were set in the present.

Instead of including a bibliography of children's books in this edition, I offer many websites and other resources where you can find carefully researched individual books as well as collections. If you can't find a book about a particular holiday, consider making one of your own. That way you will be sure to represent equally the holidays that are important to the children and families in your program.

Resources in the first edition of *Celebrate!* took a largely pre-Internet form, in the sense that they were mostly books by recognized publishers and journal articles from professional journals. What's changed dramatically since 1997 is the growth of websites produced by professional organizations, advocacy groups, government, community groups, and individuals, as well as self-published books ranging from publications online to books produced using online resources. The ease of designing and maintaining blogs has resulted in an explosion of them, as well as a constant updating and birthing of online resources.

The 2016 edition of *Celebrate!* reflects these changes: instead of a lengthy list of printed books, my resources now offer readers a guide *into* this rapidly expanding universe of materials so you can find the most appropriate books, articles, and blogs for your own classroom—or write your own, using online help.

While these revised resources may be less directly helpful than a list of recommended books, they cast a vastly wider and more intricate net than an old-fashioned resources list does.

I encourage you to choose books that meet criteria similar to mine and that reflect the needs of the particular children in your program. The books you choose should reflect the specific holidays that the children, families, and staff in your program celebrate, and how they celebrate them. They should also help meet your program's holiday goals, reflect your program's values, and follow your stated holiday policy.

Besides the terrific web resources listed below, I recommend these books as something you may want to acquire for your classroom:

National Geographic, Holidays Around the World series
Some of these wonderful books may be a bit word heavy for preschoolers, but they include lovely photos and a plethora of information about each holiday and how it is celebrated.

Kathleen T. Horning, *From Cover to Cover: Evaluating and Reviewing Children's Books*. Revised edition. New York: HarperCollins, 2010.
This user-friendly handbook has been considered a definitive guide to reading, reviewing, and critically evaluating children's books.

Recommended Internet resources offering compilations of children's books

Teaching for Change
www.tfcbooks.org
Provides a bibliography of anti-bias books for young children, including a section on holidays.

The Children's Peace Education and Anti-Bias Library
www.childpeacebooks.org/cpb/
This site has an interactive database of high-quality, developmentally appropriate books specifically for infants through five-year-olds. It includes several holiday books.

Asia for Kids
www.afk.com
This is an excellent site with lists of books, CDs, and some toys for all ages, including books about holidays. Not all books are age appropriate for preschoolers and not all meet high literary and visual art standards, but this site lists resources you cannot find anywhere else.

Cooperative Children's Book Center, University of Wisconsin–Madison
http://ccbc.education.wisc.edu/books/

This School of Education site helps librarians, teachers, child care providers, and others navigate the abundance of choices available in children's books to locate the best books possible to meet their needs. The bibliographies of children's books are listed by category, including a section on holidays.

Lee & Low Books
www.leeandlow.com
This publisher's site contains unique collections, many appropriate for children ages five and under. It includes a strong focus on multiethnic children.

Oyate
www.oyate.org
This is the best American Indian site for teachers. It was developed by members of Indian nations. It includes a list of books written by American Indians; many of these are appropriate for young children. It also provides information on how to evaluate books for anti-Indian bias.

Pinterest
www.pinterest.com
Even Pinterest has wonderful pockets of anti-bias/multicultural children's book lists, including books about holidays. Remember to use your evaluation tools and a critical eye to determine which books are appropriate for your setting.

Recommended Internet resources for evaluating children's books

To help you assess individual books for accuracy and authenticity, consult the tools below when you're making decisions about which books to use with the children and families in your program.

An Updated Guide for Selecting Anti-Bias Children's Books
www.tfcbooks.org/2013-guide-anti-bias-childrens-books
This assessment tool is an adaptation of an original publication by the Council on Interracial Books for Children, "Ten Quick Ways to Analyze Children's Books for Racism and Sexism," which became an invaluable tool for hundreds of thousands of people.

ADULTS' RESOURCES

Recommended Internet resources on holidays

Religion in the Public Schools
http://archive.adl.org/religion_ps_2004/#.VozVGZMrKt8

This publication provides a very detailed and comprehensive look at the issues of religion in all aspects of schools, including prayer, religion in the curriculum, religious displays, and more. It contains a section on teaching about religious holidays. I turn to this publication time and time again as a guide and a resource to share with others about what is allowed in public schools.

Religion in the Public Schools: Teaching about Religious Holidays
www.adl.org/assets/pdf/civil-rights/religiousfreedom/rips/RIPS-Ch6DecDil.pdf
Teachers in public programs must be careful not to cross the line between teaching about religious holidays (which is permitted) and celebrating religious holidays (which is not). This online publication is a short, readable excerpt from the more comprehensive publication *Religion in the Public Schools* by the same publisher.

The December Dilemma: Navigating Religious Holidays in the Public Schools
www.adl.org/education-outreach/education-webinars/december-dilemma.html#.VozVhpMrKt8
This is a very useful webinar addressing a myriad of considerations.

The December Dilemma: December Holiday Guidelines for Public Schools
http://archive.adl.org/issue_education/december_dilemma_2004/
A go-to document about the First Amendment and how constitutional issues apply to holidays in public schools. Includes four sections: Religion as an Educational Lesson, Holiday Assemblies, Performing Religious Music, and Decorating with Holiday Symbols.

How Can I Plan Inclusive Holiday Celebrations?
www.adl.org/assets/pdf/education-outreach/How-Can-I-Plan-Inclusive-Holiday-Celebrations.pdf
This online article from the Anti-Defamation League's Miller Early Childhood Initiative Question Corner is aimed particularly at teachers of the youngest children.

Considerations for Inclusive Holidays and Observances
www.adl.org/education-outreach/anti-bias-education/c/considerations-for-inclusive-holidays-and-observances.html#.VozVo5MrKt8
A short online piece about creating inclusive celebrations and observances.

Exploring Celebrations in Children's Services: Self-Guided Learning Package
www.gowrievictoria.org.au/app/uploads/2016/02/Exploring-Celebrations-in-Childrens-Services_Dec12.pdf

This is a self-guided training by the Australian government. Its purpose is to help learners develop an understanding of how celebrations can support children in developing awareness of and respect for diverse values and beliefs. Those who complete this package will learn to describe and implement a range of strategies to ensure that celebrations reflect the values and practices of families, children, educators, and the wider community.

Celebrating with Children: A Cultural Perspective
www.baysidefamilydaycare.com/CelebratingWithChildren-TP.pdf

A training package by the Department of Family and Community Services and the Statewide Transcultural Training and Resourcing Program in Australia designed for facilitators to use in leading a three-hour session about holidays in early learning programs. It can also be used as a self-guided training for learners.

Who's in Charge of Celebrations? A Child-Centered Approach. **AECA Resource Book Series, Volume 1, Number 1. March 1994.**
http://files.eric.ed.gov/fulltext/ED382338.pdf

Barbara Creaser and Elizabeth Dau's little booklet asks, "Who is in charge of celebrations?" and answers it from the perspective of children, parents, and staff. Alternatives to usual holiday activities are offered, and suggestions for birthdays and other everyday celebrations of childhood are included. You can access the complete text of the booklet via the link above.

Revisiting Celebrations with Young Children, **Elizabeth Dau and Kerryn Jones. Early Childhood Australia, 2004.**
http://files.eric.ed.gov/fulltext/ED488939.pdf

This is an updated version of Elizabeth Dau and Barbara Creaser's *Who's in Charge of Celebrations? A Child-Centered Approach* with sections on community celebrations, school or center celebrations, celebrations of children's learning, traditional celebrations, and more. This publication can be accessed in its entirety via the link above.

"Planning Holiday Celebrations: An Ethical Approach to Developing Policy and Practices," *Texas Child Care,* **Fall 2004: 22–31.**
www.childcarequarterly.com/pdf/fall04_holiday.pdf

Katie Campbell, Mary Jamsek, and P. D. Jolley's fantastic article is also available online. Topics include rethinking dominant culture holidays, identifying core values, ethical responsibilities, and religious celebrations in public schools. Highly recommended.

Books about general early childhood education

Carlsson-Paige, Nancy, and Diane E. Levin. *Who's Calling the Shots? How to Respond Effectively to Children's Fascination with War Play and War Toys.* Philadelphia: New Society Publishers, 1990.

Curtis, Deb, and Margie Carter. *The Art of Awareness: How Observation Can Transform Your Teaching.* Second edition. St. Paul: Redleaf Press, 2013.

————. *Designs for Living and Learning: Transforming Early Childhood Environments.* Second edition. St. Paul: Redleaf Press, 2014.

————. *Learning Together with Young Children: A Curriculum Framework for Reflective Teachers.* St. Paul: Redleaf Press, 2008.

————. *Reflecting Children's Lives: A Handbook for Planning Child-Centered Curriculum.* Second edition. St. Paul: Redleaf Press, 2011.

————. *The Visionary Director: A Handbook for Dreaming, Organizing, and Improvising in Your Center.* Second edition. St. Paul: Redleaf Press, 2010.

Edwards, Carolyn, Lella Gandini, and George Forman, editors. *The Hundred Languages of Children: The Reggio Emilia Experience in Transformation.* Third edition. New York: Praeger, 2011.

NAEYC. *Developmentally Appropriate Practice in Early Childhood Programs Serving Children from Birth through Age 8.* Third edition. Washington, DC: NAEYC, 2010.

Books on anti-bias/multicultural early education

Cronin, Sharon, and Carmen Sosa Masso. *Soy Bilingue: Language, Culture, and Young Latino Children.* Seattle: Center for Linguistic and Cultural Democracy, 2003.

Delpit, Lisa. *Other People's Children: Cultural Conflict in the Classroom.* New York: New Press, 2006.

Derman-Sparks, Louise, and the ABC Task Force. *Anti-Bias Curriculum: Tools for Empowering Young Children.* Washington, DC: NAEYC, 1989.

Derman-Sparks, Louise, and Julie Olsen Edwards. *Anti-Bias Education for Young Children and Ourselves.* Second edition. Washington, DC: NAEYC, 2010.

Derman-Sparks, Louise, Debbie Lee, and John Nimmo. *Leading Anti-Bias Early Childhood Programs: A Guide for Change.* New York: Teachers College Press, 2015.

Derman-Sparks, Louise, and Patricia G. Ramsey. *What If All the Kids Are White? Anti-Bias Multicultural Education with Young Children and Families.* Second edition. New York: Teachers College Press, 2011.

Pelo, Ann, editor. *Rethinking Early Childhood Education.* Milwaukee: Rethinking Schools, 2008.

Ramsey, Patricia G. *Teaching and Learning in a Diverse World: Multicultural Education for Young Children.* Fourth edition. New York: Teachers College Press, 2015.

Seale, Doris (Santee/Cree), Beverly Slapin, and Carolyn Silverman (Cherokee/Blackfeet), editors. *Thanksgiving: A Native Perspective.* [Available through www.oyate.org.]

Seale, Doris (Santee/Cree), and Beverly Slapin, editors. *A Broken Flute: The Native Experience in Books for Children.* Walnut Creek, CA: Alta Mira Press, and Berkeley, CA: Oyate, 2005.

Whitney, Trisha. *Kids Like Us: Using Persona Dolls in the Classroom.* St. Paul: Redleaf Press, 1999.

Wolpert, Ellen. *Start Seeing Diversity: The Basic Guide to an Anti-Bias Classroom.* St. Paul: Redleaf Press, 2005.

York, Stacey. *Roots and Wings: Affirming Culture and Preventing Bias in Early Childhood.* Third edition. St. Paul: Redleaf Press, 2016.

Books and articles about holidays

Dimidjian, Victoria Jean. "Holidays, Holy Days, and Wholly Dazed: Approaches to Special Days." *Young Children* (September 1989): 70–75.

Dorris, Michael. "Why I'm Not Thankful for Thanksgiving." *Bulletin of the Council on Interracial Books for Children* (1978): 6–9.

Gelb, Steven. "Christmas Programming in Schools: Unintended Consequences." *Childhood Education* (1987): 9–13.

Ramsey, Patricia G. "Beyond 'Ten Little Indians' and Turkeys." *Young Children* (September 1989): 28–51.

Wardle, Francis. "Bunny Ears and Cupcakes for All: Are Parties Developmentally Appropriate?" *Child Care Information Exchange* (1990): 39–41.

Books about religion

Buller, Laura. *A Faith Like Mine: A Celebration of the World's Religions through the Eyes of Children.* London and New York: DK Children, 2005.

Osborne, Mary Pope. *One World, Many Religions: The Ways We Worship.* New York: Knopf, 1996.

Appendix B:
Sample Policy and
Planning Documents

Willow Child Care Center Holiday Policy

Definition of Holiday Activities

It is important to define holiday activities because the words *holiday* and *celebration* mean different things to different people. For purposes of this holiday policy and to define our holiday practices in the classroom, we define "holiday activities" in the following way.

Holiday activities at Willow can be as simple as reading a book about a holiday and as elaborate and involved as having a party in the classroom with food, decorations, guests, and music. Activities often involve a group discussion about a holiday and how a family celebrates it, or the reading of a book about a holiday. Other times teachers set up open-ended, developmentally appropriate activities for children that relate to a holiday.

Goals and Functions of Holidays

1. To validate children's and families' holiday experiences and traditions at home

2. To expose children to different ways of celebrating the same holiday

3. To expose children to celebrations, traditions, and religions different from their own

4. To foster respect for celebrations, traditions, and religions different from children's own

5. To provide fun and a break in the routine

6. To mark time for children

7. To build a sense of community, family, and togetherness

8. To provide accurate information about holidays in a developmentally appropriate manner

9. To encourage critical thinking about bias and unfairness

10. To provide a stress-free environment

Role of Holidays in the Program

Since we plan curriculum on an emergent basis in a way that reflects children's needs and interests, the exact amount of time we spend on holidays will vary. We use children and families in the program as a barometer to help us decide how much we will do with holidays. We do have some guidelines, however, to make sure that holidays do not take over the entire curriculum. With regard to parties or actual celebrating, we will limit holiday parties to three or four per year. When we are "recognizing" a holiday (that is, having a discussion or reading a book) or providing activities related to a holiday, we might include up to five holidays per month.

For example, on the Friday before Memorial Day, we will talk about the fact that the center is closed on the following Monday and explain why, in two or three sentences. When we are doing calendar every morning, we will talk with children about holidays that just occurred or that are approaching. These recognitions of holidays, however, are no more than a two-minute discussion about what the holiday is called and what it is all about, unless children ask to know more. Similarly, when we provide activities, they will be open ended and one of many choices so they are not the focus of the entire curriculum.

How Decisions Will Be Made about Which Holidays to Include

Individual decisions about which holidays will be included will be made every year and when children and families leave or enter the program.

1. First, teachers and the director will use a variety of methods to determine what holidays are important to the children and families in the program. These methods will include a questionnaire, interviews, home visits, parent/guardian meetings, and daily communication.

2. Then teachers will make a list of any additional holidays they think are important to include. These include holidays they have incorporated in the past, social justice holidays, holidays that are celebrated by the staff, holidays that support overall classroom goals, and holidays whose stereotypes or misinformation provide opportunities for teachers to help children correct wrong impressions.

3. Next, teachers and the director will look at the holidays that children are unfamiliar with. Before deciding to include any of these holidays, teachers will make sure they can introduce them in a relevant, respectful way that connects to children's own experiences.

4. Teachers and the director will then look at the list they have generated so far and decide if anything else should be added or dropped from the list. Together they will make sure that all the chosen holidays meet at least one of the stated goals for holidays and that none of those holidays will offend or hurt any child or family.

How Holidays Will Be Implemented in the Curriculum

Below is a list of general guidelines we follow at Willow as we implement holidays:

1. We are inclusive. We strive to validate everyone and exclude no one. We pay attention to the balance and the importance we put on certain holidays over others. No one holiday is portrayed as more important than any other.

2. We concentrate on reflecting a holiday in a way that is important and relevant to families at home.

3. We work to be culturally relevant in all of our activities. We portray holidays from the point of view of the person or group that celebrates those holidays. If teachers

are not of the religious or cultural group that celebrates a certain holiday, we gather information from books and people who celebrate the holiday.

4. We do our own research. Teachers learn what they can about a family's holiday that we are unfamiliar with before asking that family to supply information. This communicates respect and a genuine desire to obtain information.

5. We involve families as much as possible in the implementation of holiday activities and celebrations. We also keep families informed of upcoming holiday activities and events.

6. We are careful to avoid stereotypes when presenting holiday information to children, putting up decorations, and implementing activities. We also are committed to addressing unfairness in holiday images and messages that children may be experiencing outside of the classroom so they learn to recognize bias and hurtfulness.

7. We provide activities that are developmentally appropriate for the ages and stages of the children. Young children need concrete, hands-on activities and simple explanations. We are careful not to abandon all we know about good practices when it comes to holiday activities. We know that teacher-directed art and reproducible crafts that all look alike do not foster creativity or individual expression.

8. We are sympathetic to the fact that holiday time can create hardships for some families because of financial constraints, family problems, and so on. We are careful not to implement any activities that put financial pressure on families.

How Religious Aspects of Holidays Will Be Approached

While teachers won't teach the religious aspect of a holiday or teach one religion or religious holiday as the correct one, we will explain, in a developmentally appropriate way, what the historical meaning of that holiday is if children ask us directly for that information. Religious aspects will be explained matter-of-factly, in simple language. Families will be consulted for the actual language they use when talking about religious holidays to their children. Children will also be referred back to their families for more explanation and in-depth information about religious aspects of holidays. Aside from providing answers to children's direct questions about the religious aspects of holidays, teachers in general will avoid talking about religion without sacrificing the underlying meaning of a holiday. For example, we will explain that Christmas is a time for giving and sharing and Valentine's Day is a day for friendship and caring.

Plan to Work with Children and Families Who Don't Celebrate Some or Any Holidays

We will not celebrate any individual holiday that excludes one or more children. If we have children in the program who do not celebrate any holidays, we will work with all families and staff to come up with a plan for holidays that meet their children's needs so they are not left out.

How We Will Evaluate the Effectiveness of Holiday Activities

We will be constantly reflective of holiday activities we have done in the past and how we might handle holidays in the future. Once a year, teachers, the director, and families will get together to talk about what is working, what isn't working, and to discuss future strategies.

Epiphany Early Learning Preschool Holiday Policy

Goals for Holiday Activities at Epiphany Early Learning Preschool (EELP)

To promote connection among children, families, and staff

At EELP we are committed to authentic relationships and to genuine community. Recognition of holidays can bring people together in warmth and togetherness and build and strengthen connections between home and school. They also can promote a sense of community among children as they learn about one another's holidays and participate in activities together. It is our hope that holidays will help to link home and EELP in meaningful ways.

To support, validate, and represent the experiences of children, their families, and staff in the program

Clearly one of the most important reasons to include holidays in our curriculum is because they are such important and meaningful events in the lives of so many of the children and families at EELP. It is our goal that holiday activities at EELP support children's experiences at home and in their communities. We hope to give all children the message that what is important in their families is valid and worthwhile and worth mention at school. We aim to make children's families a visible, tangible presence in our classrooms. This is particularly important for children and families whose holidays are generally not reflected in the media, in store decorations, in children's books, and in mainstream society in general.

To offer another opportunity for learning in a developmentally appropriate way

Holiday activities and discussions can enrich and inform the lives of children. They provide an avenue for children and adults to learn about the important events in their own and many other people's lives. Holiday activities can also be perfect opportunities for children to learn in a hands-on way. Making decorations, baking, singing, creating, sharing, and storytelling are activities that help our senses come alive with smells, tastes, sights, sounds, and things to touch.

To celebrate both similarities and differences in children's lives

Holidays are another opportunity to learn about the ways that we are similar to and different from one another. They can show children in direct, meaningful ways that the same holidays can be celebrated differently, and that people often celebrate holidays honoring events and beliefs unique to their ethnic or cultural groups. Through conversation about differences and similarities we can deepen the ways in which we know one another and grow our community. Activities can also help children see the similar themes that run through many different holidays, such as death, renewal, light and darkness, liberation, and harvest.

To mark time for children and encourage awareness of natural rhythms in the seasons and in life

Holiday celebrations can underscore certain times of the year by celebrating beginnings, endings, and other significant rhythms, such as seasonal changes. By bringing holidays and other rituals that happen only once a year into our curriculum, we allow a break in the regular routine of full-day, year-round child care where exceptions and special fun are the norm for a day or two.

To support children's connection to family and their cultural roots

Holiday rituals can reaffirm or deepen connection to cultural roots, helping to teach or remind children of who they and their families are. These rituals can also give children a sense of security. They feel comfort in knowing that they will see some familiar sights, taste some familiar foods, and be together with people who are important to them. By including or talking about these same holiday rituals in the classroom, those reminders and feelings of comfort can be found at EELP as well.

To stretch children's awareness and empathy

Many different kinds of holidays celebrated, and they are all special and wonderful for the families who celebrate them. It is our goal at EELP to craft an approach to holidays that reflects the children and families in our program and that acknowledges the wider world in which we live. By learning about holidays that are different from their own, children become aware of other people's ways of living. This can help children learn that what and how they celebrate isn't the one "right" or only way.

To teach children critical thinking about bias

Holidays are an opportunity to live our commitment to anti-bias practices at EELP. Since many holiday images and messages from television, videos, store decorations, and children's books unfortunately portray gender, race, culture, class, and historical bias, including these holidays in the curriculum provides opportunities to teach children how to examine what they see and hear for messages that are unfair or hurtful. Activities and discussions can also challenge children to consider the commercialization and mass marketing of certain holidays. These activities can lead children to understand that the inability to afford items, or choosing not to purchase them, doesn't make a family bad or "less" than other families.

To teach children about social justice and activism

Empowering children to stand up for themselves and others is one of the cornerstone goals of an anti-bias approach. By discussing and sharing social justice holidays such as Passover, Martin Luther King Jr.'s birthday, and Mexican Independence Day, children learn about what real people struggled over in the past to create a better life for themselves and others. These activities can lead to discussions about people who are working for justice today.

To have fun

Holiday activities, conversation, and sharing can be fun. They add spice to daily life and bring excitement, anticipation, magic, joy, and laughter into the classroom.

Implementation

Nuts and bolts

- In general, our approach to holidays is one of recognition and discussion rather than celebration, as in parties and candy and large get-togethers.

- When we bring holiday-related curriculum to the classroom, we ensure that the activities are developmentally appropriate.

- We provide for play about holidays.

- We incorporate and take advantage of opportunities to learn about science— through pumpkins cut open and decomposing, changing colors of leaves, and so on.

- We focus on underlying themes of particular holidays. (For example, with Halloween, we focus on dressing up, disguising ourselves, and playing tricks, and with Thanksgiving, we focus on ways our families come together to reflect on what we are thankful for.)

- We focus on the elements of a holiday that will grow our community, which is often the sharing of stories.

- We also celebrate birthdays, new births, comings, and goings.

- If we find ourselves faced with including a holiday that we are not familiar with, we will do our own research in the library, on the Internet, by reading children's books, by consulting a community center, and by talking to colleagues and community members who celebrate that particular holiday to ensure that we have accurate information.

Connection to seasonal changes and rhythms

- We maintain a connection to seasons and natural rhythms.

- Our thoughts and commitments around the seasonal cycles are broader than any particular holiday.

- We weave the natural world into our classrooms.

- We nurture children's relationships with the natural world.

- We honor the rhythms of the seasons.

- Our curriculum practices often center on the natural world, as we notice the changes in weather, lightness, and darkness.

- We may have nature tables or seasonal tables in our classroom.

How we work in partnership with families

- We aim to make home/school connections permeable.

- We strive to bring home into the school by bringing in holidays.

- We send invitations to families throughout the year to help us celebrate holidays.

- We invite families to participate by bringing in specific family traditions.

- We honor each family's contribution—listening, acknowledging, demonstrating respect, and asking questions.

- We gather holiday memories from families by asking families, for example, to "bring a clue about something you did while on vacation," or "bring something that helps you tell a story about your winter break," and "after Halloween please bring in pictures of your children in their costumes." Or we send home blank posters or boxes inviting families to fill them with vacation/holiday memories.

- We will work closely with families who celebrate a holiday we are not familiar with to ensure that we understand not just what the holiday is about but also exactly how this particular family celebrates it.

Anti-bias practices

- We bring out the inherent anti-bias and diversity themes in an intentional way.

- We seize the opportunities to talk about similarities and differences in holidays and how we celebrate or don't.

- In the preschool rooms, we talk directly about stereotypes in holidays. For example, we help kids think critically about stereotypical images of American Indians at Thanksgiving (and year-round) and older women at Halloween (and year-round).

Balance

- We intentionally don't allow one or all holidays to take over the curriculum or our days with children.

- We carefully plan so that holiday activities or conversations don't take over an entire day, week, or month.

- We create our own EELP traditions and seasonal celebrations.

- We create a safe haven from the overload that children receive outside of school.

- We have a seasonal emphasis on holidays.

- We weave holidays into the ongoing life of our classrooms, rather than stopping what and how we do our daily practices to focus on a holiday or holidays.

- In general, we steer away from holiday parties in the classroom.

Nonsecular and inclusive

- We use "some people believe . . ." when talking about a particular holiday or celebration so children don't assume that everyone celebrates a particular holiday or in a particular way.

- We don't promote any particular holiday.

- We create opportunities for children to bring their family experiences around holidays into our classrooms in ways that are respectful of a range of practices and beliefs.

Religion

- We try to observe holidays in a secular way but may briefly and generally explain the religious story behind a holiday.

- While we focus on the secular aspects of a holiday, we try to do that without sacrificing the underlying meaning of a holiday.

- We are careful not to promote any religion or any holiday as the "right" one.

- We use the phrase "some people believe . . ."

- We answer children's questions simply and matter-of-factly and refer them to their families for more information.

- We don't stop a child's singing or storytelling about holidays.

Commercialism

- We avoid activities that may put a financial strain on any family.

- We talk to children about advertising and marketing in ways that make sense to them in order to teach them that companies that sell products do whatever they can to make you want to buy.

- We focus on the underlying meaning of a holiday as being about "being thankful" or "sharing" or "giving," rather than "receiving lots and lots of presents."

How We Choose Holidays

We will gather information from families about what holidays and special days are important in their families and how they celebrate them.

We might do this by

- inviting families to a meeting to share information about what holidays they celebrate at home;

- putting out a survey asking for information about what and how families celebrate;

- having informal conversations with families at drop off/pickup and at other appropriate times to ask for information about holidays in their families.

We will work closely with families to build trust and assure them that we will use their information respectfully and appropriately, particularly when families are hesitant to share personal information about holidays and other family and cultural practices for fear that it will make their child look "different."

We will ask families to share not only *what* they celebrate but also *how* they celebrate each holiday.

Introduce holidays that are not celebrated by enrolled families to increase awareness

- We'll bring in holidays that the teachers and other staff at EELP celebrate, especially if they are holidays that are unfamiliar to the children.

- Next we'll look to the community outside of EELP and bring in a handful of holidays throughout the year that introduce diversity. We'll do this in a way that connects to children's own experiences and understandings.

Holidays that we plan to include no matter what

- We will include holidays, celebrations, rituals, and events that have become a part of EELP culture, such as the celebration of births, deaths, birthdays, comings, and goings.

- We will include holidays that portray stereotypes or misinformation to help children learn critical thinking skills.

- We will bring in social justice holidays in order to expose children to people who have worked for social justice.

Considerations

- We won't assume that a person from a particular ethnic or cultural group celebrates a certain holiday. For example, we won't assume that every African American person celebrates Kwanzaa.

- We will plan carefully and intentionally so that we include a balance of holidays from specific religious and cultural groups and create a balance of national holidays and other holidays.

- We will ensure that at least one holiday is represented from every family enrolled in our discussions and activities.

- We will bring in holidays so that everyone in the program is represented.

- We will make careful decisions about whether or not to include holidays that are celebrated by one child in the classroom in order to avoid making them feel like a "token" or the "spokesperson" for their group.

- We will educate ourselves about holidays we don't know about so we don't present misinformation or stereotypical images or ideas.

Holiday Evaluation Questionnaire for Families

Dear Families,

It's time for us to take a look at how effective our holiday practices have been throughout the past year. Your input is critical to our evaluation process, and we would greatly appreciate it if you would answer the following questions and return the questionnaire to the office by next Monday.

1. Are you satisfied with our overall approach to holidays this past year? Please tell us why or why not.

2. What would you like us to add to our practices?

3. What would you like us to stop doing?

4. Did our activities and discussions this year adequately and accurately reflect your child and your family's rituals and celebrations? If so, how? If not, how can we improve?

5. Do you feel that there were enough opportunities for you to become involved in our activities? If not, how can we improve in this area?

6. What suggestions do you have for us in the next year?

° * ⚹ ✳⚹ ✳ * ⚹ * ∞ * * ⚹ ✳⚹ * * ∞ °

Family Questionnaire about Holidays

Dear Families,

Your answers to the following questions will help us greatly in our efforts to develop an inclusive, sensitive approach to holiday celebrations and to plan activities appropriate for your children's ages and developmental levels. Thank you for taking the time to fill this out. Please return it to the office by [*date*].

1. On a scale of 1 to 10, how important are holidays to your family? (The number 1 means unimportant and 10 means extremely important.)

2. What special days do you celebrate in your family? How do you celebrate them?

3. How would you like the program to support or reflect your celebrations? If your family does not celebrate any holidays, how would you prefer us to work with you and your child if/when we have holiday activities in our program?

4. What would you like your child to gain from holiday activities while in our program?

5. What concerns do you have about holiday activities?

6. How do you feel about your child learning about or participating in holiday activities that are not part of your family's tradition? Are there any holidays you would object to?

7. Religion plays an important role in many holidays. While considering these next questions, please keep in mind that our teachers would not teach any religious perspective as the "right" religion; rather we would always say, "Some people believe . . ." or "At Sally's house, they believe . . ."

8. What religious holidays, if any, do you celebrate in your home?

9. How would you feel about your child experiencing in our program the religious aspects of holidays you celebrate in your family?

10. How would you feel about your child being exposed to religious aspects of a holiday that your family may not believe in?

11. How would you like to participate in holiday activities in the classroom?

∘ * ✳ ✶✱✶ ✱ * * ∞ * * ✱ ✶✱✶ ✱ * * ∘

Holiday Practices Improvement Plan

What went really well?

What could be improved?

What changes will we make next time?

References

Booze, ReGena. 1988. "Incorporating the Principles of Kwanzaa into Your Daily Curriculum: A Handbook for Teachers of Young Children." Unpublished master's thesis, Pacific Oaks College, Pasadena, CA.

Carlsson-Paige, Nancy, and Diane E. Levin. 1990. *Who's Calling the Shots? How to Respond Effectively to Children's Fascination with War Play and War Toys.* Philadelphia: New Society Publishers.

Carter, Margie. 2010. "Looking for Core Values." *Exchange,* Sept–Oct 2010: 18–21.

Carter, Margie, and Deb Curtis. 2009. *The Visionary Director: A Handbook for Dreaming, Organizing, and Improvising in Your Center.* 2nd ed. St. Paul, MN: Redleaf Press.

Derman-Sparks, Louise, and The ABC Task Force. 1989. *Anti-Bias Curriculum: Tools for Empowering Young Children.* 1st ed. Washington, DC: National Association for the Education of Young Children.

Derman-Sparks, Louise, and Julie Olsen Edwards. 2010. *Anti-Bias Education for Young Children and Ourselves.* 2nd ed. Washington, DC: National Association for the Education of Young Children.

George, Jean Craighead. 1993. *Dear Rebecca, Winter Is Here.* New York: HarperTrophy.

King County Office of Performance, Strategy, and Budget. 2013. "King County's Changing Demographics: A View of Our Increasing Diversity." June 5, 2013. http://www.kingcounty.gov/~/media/exec/PSB/documents/AGR/KingCountyDemographics2012.ashx?la=en.

Migration Policy Institute. 2016. "Frequently Requested Statistics on Immigrants and Immigration in the United States, April 14, 2016." Jie Zong and Jeanne Batalova, eds. http://www.migrationpolicy.org/article/frequently-requested-statistics-immigrants-and-immigration-united-states.

Rappaport, Doreen. 2001. *Martin's Big Words: The Life of Dr. Martin Luther King, Jr.* New York: Hyperion.

Stone, Jane Davis. 1991. "A Jehovah's Witness Perspective on Holiday Curriculum." Unpublished master's thesis, Pacific Oaks College, Pasadena, CA.

Whitney, Trisha. 1999. *Kids Like Us: Using Persona Dolls in the Classroom.* St. Paul: Redleaf Press.